"*Get Backed* is the essential guide to launching a company—not only raising money, but also raising relationships. If you're a founder or an entrepreneur, this book has the tools you need to succeed."

—**ADAM GRANT**, Professor of Management, the Wharton School; *New York Times* bestselling author, *Give and Take*

"This book delivers completely new and refreshing ideas on how to raise money and build genuine relationships with investors."

—**DAVID COHEN**, cofounder and Managing Partner, Techstars

"The best way to solve the world's most pressing problems is to start a company. This book shows you how."

—**JOHN MACKEY**, cofounder and Co-CEO, Whole Foods Market; coauthor, *Conscious Capitalism*

"The ability to get a startup funded is a crucial test for a founder. It pulls together all of the larger requirements of the job—crafting a clear vision, laying out a clear execution path, and cultivating relationships above money. Evan Baehr and Evan Loomis have created a field guide to help the best founders get the funding they deserve for their disruptive ideas."

—**MIKE MAPLES JR.**, cofounder and Partner, Floodgate; investor, Twitter

"Even the best business pl well. Read this book to m

—**BLAKE MASTERS**, cofounder, Judicata, coauthor (with Peter Thiel), *Zero to One*

"Successful companies grow out of strong communities. This guide helps you raise friends, partners, and investors—the ultimate community to make your venture succeed."

—**TOMMY LEEP**, Chief Connector, Rothenberg Ventures

"Founders envision how the world can be different—and invite others to join that vision by telling stories of hope, failure, triumph, and a better future. *Get Backed* is the definitive primer on how founders ought to tell these stories."

—**JAMES K. A. SMITH**, Professor of Philosophy, Calvin College; author, *Desiring the Kingdom*

"Finally, a book by people who have actually done it! *Get Backed* is a staple for any startup library. It was our handbook for raising capital for our venture—and it will do the same for you!"

—**LAURA and BEN HARRISON**, cofounders, Jonas Paul Eyewear

GET
BACKED

GET BACKED

CRAFT YOUR STORY | BUILD THE PERFECT PITCH DECK | LAUNCH THE VENTURE OF YOUR DREAMS

EVAN BAEHR | **EVAN LOOMIS**

HARVARD BUSINESS REVIEW PRESS

BOSTON, MASSACHUSETTS

HBR Press Quantity Sales Discounts

Harvard Business Review Press titles are available at significant quantity discounts when purchased in bulk for client gifts, sales promotions, and premiums. Special editions, including books with corporate logos, customized covers, and letters from the company or CEO printed in the front matter, as well as excerpts of existing books, can also be created in large quantities for special needs.

For details and discount information for both print and ebook formats, contact booksales@harvardbusiness.org, tel. 800-988-0886, or www.hbr.org/bulksales.

Library of Congress Cataloging-in-Publication Data

Baehr, Evan.
   Get backed : the handbook for creating your pitch deck, raising money, and launching the venture of your dreams / Evan Baehr and Evan Loomis.
      pages   cm
   ISBN 978-1-63369-072-1 (alk. paper)
   1. New business enterprises—Finance.   2. New business enterprises—Management.   3. Entrepreneurship.   I. Loomis, Evan.   II. Title.
   HG4027.6.B24   2015
   658.15'224—dc23

                                                            2015015748

When your relationship with your spouse is strong, you move out into the world in strength no matter how tumultuous it is, explains theologian Tim Keller. But when that relationship is weak, you move out into the world in weakness, even if everything seems to be going perfectly.

As residents of a tumultuous world, we dedicate this work to our spouses, Kristina and Brandi, who—like so many spouses of entrepreneurs—sacrificed eternally by making ends meet, putting the kids to bed alone, and shouldering way more than half of the work at home.

And despite the burdens they bore, they often looked us right in the eyes during entrepreneurship's darkest moments and said, "I believe in you." And that belief alone equipped us to move out into the world with great strength.

—Evan Baehr and Evan Loomis
  Austin, TX

Contents

Acknowledgments

We are truly grateful to all those who have assisted with this project, and we'd like to express our sincere thanks for the generous help and support we've received along the way.

This book would not have happened without Trevor Boehm's tireless work and creativity. He served as our quarterback, led the writing and research efforts, and conducted countless interviews. Our names are on the cover, but Trevor is the true hero of *Get Backed*.

We'd also like to express our deepest gratitude to Harvard Business Review Press. Our first e-mail from Tim Sullivan, editorial director at the Press, said, "The good news is that I took the project to our acquisitions meeting this morning. The better news is that the committee was wildly enthusiastic about the book—and how often can you say that any committee is wildly enthusiastic about anything?" From the get-go, the Press has been a joy to work with, and we are deeply indebted to Tim for believing in us and seeing the importance of a book like this. We are especially grateful to a few folks on his team, namely, Jennifer Waring, Stephani Finks, Julie Devoll, Kevin Evers, and Nina Nocciolino.

Showing your investor pitch deck to strangers is a bit like giving the world a key to your front door. It is courageous and an extreme act of generosity. Most of the entrepreneurs we interviewed simply said, "No, you cannot publish my pitch deck . . . are you crazy?" It is for that reason that we are so grateful to the thirteen founders who said "Yes": Brad McNamara, Cofounder and CEO, Freight Farms; George Arison, Founder and CEO, Shift; Jonathan

Beekman, Founder and CEO, Man Crates; Justin McLeod, Founder and CEO, Hinge; Kegan Schouwenburg, Founder and CEO, SOLS Systems; McKay Thomas, Cofounder and CEO, First Opinion; Michael McDaniel, Founder and CEO, Reaction, Inc.; Russ Heddleston, Cofounder and CEO, DocSend; Ryan Allis, Cofounder and Chairman, Connect; Steven van Wel, Cofounder and CEO, Karma; Wade Eyerly, Cofounder and CEO, Beacon; Zvi Band, Cofounder and CEO, Contactually; and Will Haughey, Cofounder and Chief Blockhead, Tegu.

A few other people without whom this labor of love simply would not have been possible: Curtis Eggemeyer, CEO of Lemi Shine, who gave us a lot of encouragement and the seed capital needed to continue our work. A book is quite possibly the worst investment you can make, so we're hopeful that *Get Backed* provides social returns for Curtis; Steve Nelson, at Harvard Business School, who first introduced us to Tim Sullivan; Charlie Hoehn and Tucker Max for their marketing genius; Erin at Able Lending and Lori of 33Vincent for taking care of the small details so we could keep our sights set on the bigger picture; Steven Tomlinson, who opened our imaginations to the idea of "play"; Steven Eggert, former designer at frog, who took on the first designs of the book; Dave Blanchard, Josh Kwan, Jon Hart, Jason Locy, Jon Tyson, and Dr. Steve Graves—our dear friends at Praxis who provided friendship, insight, and encouragement along the way; Francis Pedraza, our hero of the Friendship Loop, for allowing us to dig into his methodology and crack the code on relationship fundraising; Mike Rothenberg, Founder, Rothenberg Ventures, who made countless introductions to founders of startups along the way; Jason Bornhorst, Founder and CEO, Filament Labs; Will Sauer, Director of Finance and Operations, Skycatch; Sanjay Dastoor, Cofounder, Boosted Boards; Adam Tichauer, former President and CEO, Playbutton; Deena Varshavskaya, Founder and CEO, Wanelo; Jeff Avallon, Cofounder, IdeaPaint; Jason Seats, Partner, Techstars; Scott Harrison, Founder, charity: water; Dan Martell, Founder, Clarity.fm; Nancy Duarte, author, *slide:ology*; Tommy Leep, Chief Connector, Rothenberg Ventures; and Chi-Hua Chien, venture capitalist, Goodwater Capital, and Twitter, Facebook, and Spotify investor.

Evan Loomis would also like to thank:

Mom and Dad for always saying "go for it" and funding every crazy startup idea I've had—from lawn mowing to pressure washing and even wedding videography (what the heck was I thinking? I was terrible). I'll pay you guys back soon … Yes, soon … I promise …

Former President George H. W. Bush for inviting me to serve as his assistant during college. Watching him genuinely care for people and write countless handwritten notes humbled me and helped me understand why he was one of the most powerful people in the world.

Former US Secretary of Defense Robert Gates and senior lecturer Jim Olson, two former cold war spies and professors at Texas A&M University, for casually suggesting that

I look into investment banking after graduation. Their counsel changed the course of my life.

Ian Sugarman, now Vice Chairman of Retail Investment Banking at Morgan Stanley, for giving me my first job on Wall Street. Ian meticulously taught me how to create pitch decks and helped me realize that I love people more than cubicles and Microsoft Excel.

Scott Erwin, an American hero and friend, who got shot in Iraq, almost died, and lived to complete an Ironman Triathlon and swim the English Channel. He constantly inspires me to dream bigger and keep going when I get knocked down.

Dr. Steven Garber and Mark Rodgers, my former colleagues at Wedgwood Circle, for showing me how to advance "goodness, truth, and beauty for the common good" through the critical sectors of media and entertainment.

Judi McQueary, my aunt and boss at Corinthian, for being the very first investor in TreeHouse at a time when there was nothing but the proverbial notes on a napkin. But I'm most thankful for her friendship, laughter, and joyful spirit.

My cofounders and investors at TreeHouse, for teaching me everything I know about startups and giving their hearts and souls to get our first store launched: Jason Ballard, Kevin Graham, Paul Yanosy, Peter Ackerson, and Brian Williamson. Simply put, TreeHouse would have been a pipe dream without a few key investors backing us: Garrett Boone, Cofounder, The Container Store; Greg King, former President, Valero Energy Corporation; Bruce Hill, private investor and co-owner, San Antonio Spurs; Justin Cox, Partner, Cox Partners; Thomas Lehrman, Founder, Haystack Partners; Brad Allen, private investor. You're all mentors and I'm thankful for your wisdom.

The last section of the book, titled "Introduction to the Friendship Loop," would have been hollow without my closest friends, who embody true friendship. C.S. Lewis said that "Friendship is the greatest of worldly goods," and I could not agree more. Here are the people who have made me better simply by being my friends: Taylor Jackson, Dave Thompson, Jason Ballard, Jonathan Lusk, Jared Fuson, Yobany Mayen, Trevor Brock, Jon Wolfshohl, David Hollon, Ryan Nixon, Brent Baker, Brad Dunn, Will Haughey, Brock Dahl, Hunter Grunden, Sean Clifford, David Vennett, Justin Yarborough, Dave Blanchard, Duncan Sahner, Clayton Christopher, Reese Ryan, Jay Kleberg, David Mebane, Jeff Harbach, Brian Haley, Curtis Eggemeyer, Kevin Robnett, Noah Riner, Jared Jonker, Kevin Patterson, AJ Gafford, Kevin Peterson, Derick Thompson, Sly Majid, Trey Arbuckle, and Tim Cleveland.

Evan Baehr would also like to thank:

Ms. Hess, my high school debate coach, who taught me the basics of speech and rhetoric and embedded in me my lifelong passion for communication.

Kenny Trout, for creating Excel Communications, giving me my first chance to sell something—and yes, it was door-to-door long-distance phone service.

Kate Reilly, my Princeton college debate partner, with whom I disagree on nearly every possible topic . . . which, of course, made us unstoppable.

Robert George and Cornel West, two Princeton professors who teach the world that two men of goodwill but diverging opinions not only can but must have civil discourse to advance the cause of humanity.

My cofounder, Will Davis, who puts up with my antics and is always a source of encouragement. Will extended perhaps the most generous invitation to me five years ago when he said, "I want to do this with you because I know that if something ever happened to me you'd care for my family." And I absolutely would.

Tony Deifell, who introduced me to one of the biggest and most important questions of my life: "Why do you do what you do?"

Sheryl Sandberg, who introduced me to Mark Zuckerberg by saying, "Evan is the only person I've ever hired because he asks great questions."

Peter Thiel, whose intellectual rigor demands answers to questions such as: "What is something you believe that no one else does?"

Mike Maples, our first major investor, who has been the ultimate supporter and encourager at every turn, and who commented after our Series A: "You could sell ice to Eskimos."

Dylan Hogarty, who was the first person to ever say, "You know, you might actually want to try out this entrepreneurship thing."

And finally to Dave Crabbe, Brett Gibson, Joel Bryce, Will Davis, Mark Gundersen, and Mike Lage: You inspire, congratulate, coach, and help me become the person I was made to be.

The achievement of this publication is as much for each of you as it is for us. Thank you, thank you!

GET
BACKED

Introduction

by Evan Loomis

Fundraising for my startup almost wrecked my marriage.

Every Monday morning, I would fly out of Dulles Airport and crisscross the country to pitch my dream of a new, sustainable, home improvement store to potential investors.

The weeks and months dragged on. The dream started to unravel.

Investors committed, only to bail months later because the process was taking too long. My friends sent e-mails with subject lines like, "Are you alive???" It was even worse at home.

A creeping separation had started to set in between my wife and me. We were spending too much time away from each other. Our love was icing over. Our lives were diverging, and I hated the direction in which mine was headed.

I knew a lot about raising money. After college, I worked as an investment banker on Wall Street, where I sold mega-companies like Burger King to private equity firms. I had analyzed hundreds, if not thousands, of deals. When I left New York, I cofounded an angel investment group in DC. I knew what investors wanted because I was one of them. Every day I received e-mails from people looking for tips on fundraising. I was the fundraising guy.

And yet, here I was, two years into launching TreeHouse Home Improvement, with a third of my $7.5 million round left to close in the worst housing crisis in US history. It felt like Bill Murray's 1993 classic *Groundhog Day*. In every meeting, I relived the same maddening defeat over and over again. A few friends had the courage to tell me that the dream needed to die.

In November 2010, I finally admitted that there was no way I could close the remainder of the round. This e-mail was my white flag of surrender:

Date: Tuesday, November 9, 2010

Subject: TreeHouse Update

Dear Friends and Investors:

Over two years ago, we started off with a unique vision to launch a green home improvement store called TreeHouse that would make sustainable building easy, accessible, and fun . . . As you know, we have hit some roadblocks that have kept us from getting the necessary funding for our first store.

With this in mind, here are a few options our team has considered:

KEEP PUSHING. Under this scenario, our team would keep pushing to lock down the remaining investment capital. In our opinion, and while our emotions and courage want to walk this path, this is not the right choice. It is not sustainable to our team financially, it stretches our credibility and good word with partners, and it fails to acknowledge the current situation.

THROW IN THE TOWEL. This scenario would dissolve the idea, team, and legal entity. We do not believe this is the right course either. One of the consistent points of feedback from our investors and partners is "This is a great idea. Someone will eventually do it, but the timing for the launch may be off."

TEMPORARILY PUT THE BUSINESS IN HIBERNATION. In light of a great business concept and potentially bad timing, we think that putting TreeHouse in hibernation is the right course of action. It allows us to preserve all the intellectual, relational, and financial capital that has been poured into the business, and wait on alert for better timing.

This decision was not reached in haste, or without a lot of consideration. We look forward to discussing or answering any questions with you over the phone, but wanted to make sure communication got out in a timely manner, so you are released to take any steps you need to take.

Again, we are proud to call you partners and friends, and we will continue to keep you informed of any developments. Many sincere thanks on behalf of the entire TreeHouse team, and as always, please do not hesitate to call us with any questions.

Best, Evan

I had failed. We were done.

Then, a miracle happened. Two weeks after that e-mail went out, I got a call from Greg King, one of my investors. "TreeHouse needs to come off the shelf," he said. He would help us raise the remaining $3 million.

Within thirty days, we had closed the round.

How Do You Launch the Venture of Your Dreams?

Sixty-three percent of today's American twenty-somethings want to start a business.* By 2020, there will be an estimated billion entrepreneurs worldwide. Whether it's the next Facebook, the next world-changing nonprofit, or the next coffee shop down the street, starting something is *the* ambition of today's generation.

But here's the dirty little secret: starting something is insanely hard.

Launching the venture of your dreams takes more hustle, more failure, and significantly more resources than a lot of people can stomach. Yet, talk to any entrepreneurs who've been through it and they will tell you one thing: it's worth it.

*Minda Zetlin, "Survey: 63% of 20-Somethings Want to Start a Business," *Inc.*, December 17, 2013, http://www.inc.com/minda-zetlin/63-percent-of-20-somethings-want-to-own-a-business.html; and "An Entrepreneurial Generation of 18- to 34-Year-Olds Wants to Start Companies When the Economy Rebounds, According to New Poll," Ewing Marion Kauffman Foundation, November 10, 2011, http://www.kauffman.org/newsroom/2012/11/an-entrepreneurial-generation-of-18-to-34yearolds-wants-to-start-companies-when-economy-rebounds-according-to-new-poll.

The purpose of this book is to demystify one of the most intimidating parts of launching a venture: raising money.

Seriously? Another Book on Fundraising?

There's no shortage of advice on fundraising. Most of it is terrible.

Self-described experts spout phrases like, "create a business plan," "show traction," and "create urgency," without any practical insight into how to do what they suggest. A great strategy for a serial entrepreneur with a track record of success will likely be the worst possible advice for a first-time founder. Experienced entrepreneurs forget what raising money is like when you have no network, no track record, and, at best, only a conceptual knowledge of a term sheet. The entrepreneurs we know aren't interested in the theoretical best way to do something; they are interested in what works. That's why we (Evan Baehr and Evan Loomis, longtime friends) wrote this book. We wanted to give entrepreneurs what we wished we had had when raising money for our ventures.

There's a big gap between what experienced entrepreneurs like giving out as advice and the specific circumstances in which young entrepreneurs are operating.

—*Deena Varshavskaya,*
founder and CEO, Wanelo

Over the last two years, we mentored dozens of first-time founders and interviewed angel investors, venture capitalists, directors of angel networks, heads of family investment offices, and CEOs of crowdfunding platforms. We took improv classes. We infiltrated some of the country's biggest accelerators and angel groups, and sweet-talked fifteen successful entrepreneurs into letting us show you exactly what they did to raise money, including the pitch decks they showed investors. We're excited to write this book because we have done this and are doing it now. In the middle of writing this book one of us scored a $100 million business deal and one of us raised $25 million, which included the second-largest round ever raised on the startup platform AngelList at the time. We did all of these things to answer one question: *What does it really take to raise money?*

The Secret to Raising Money

What we discovered is that the skill to raise the money you need, get expert feedback, and build partnerships isn't just an X factor that some people have and others don't. On the contrary, it can be decoded.

There are specific habits and tools that aspiring entrepreneurs can cultivate to dramatically increase the likelihood that their ventures will succeed. We give you those skills and tools here.

In the next several chapters, you will:

- Study the original pitch decks of startups that raised wildly successful funding rounds.

- Access templates for common pitch deck elements, like identifying the problem, showing your solution, and distinguishing yourself from the competition.

- Find out which kind of capital to raise from which people.

- See e-mail scripts and techniques to get a meeting with absolutely anyone, including angel investors, venture capitalists, and potential board members.

Yet, as helpful as these techniques are, they are not the secret to raising money.

Nearly every startup founder we interviewed had a "miracle" like the TreeHouse story you just read about—some unexpected occurrence that catapulted him or her into ultimate success. As we dug in, we discovered that these miracles weren't really miraculous at all; they were the direct result of relationships the founders had nurtured earlier. For Loomis, his friendship with Greg King caused Greg to put his own reputation on the line to help Loomis close TreeHouse's funding round.

The secret to raising money is one simple principle: successful fundraisers don't raise money, they raise friends.

Friendships Matter

We want you to crush it with your startup. But even more than that, we want you to build friendships that outlast any term sheet and create true value for you, your community, and your venture. The different strategies for fundraising will come and go. Market dynamics, industry trends, and timing make each venture's fundraising journey uncharted territory. Yet, the one constant across every startup, every industry, every moment since the beginning of human life on earth is the value of meaningful relationships. This book is really about challenging people to move their visions for the future further down the field by surrounding themselves with like-minded brothers and sisters who believe in what they are doing. Along the way, you may just find yourself with access to more cash than you need.

Part One: Create Your Pitch

Part one is all about the pitch. It starts by introducing you to the pitch deck, why people make them, and why they matter. Chapter 1 describes the birth of the pitch deck. Chapter 2 outlines the key building blocks of a deck: ten key slides you should start with. Then, chapters 3 through 5 focus in detail on three elements of your pitch deck and pitching in general: story, design, and words. Chapter 6 is devoted entirely to the pitch decks that have successfully raised money, and chapter 7 offers some practical exercises for improving your pitching muscle.

Part Two: Get Backed

Part two is all about the fundraising process. Chapter 8 is an introduction to startup finance 101—how funding rounds work, the difference between debt and equity, and an overview of basic terms in an agreement. Chapter 9 describes which kinds of investors fund which kinds of companies. Chapters 10 through 13 are the culmination of everything else in the book—a simple but powerful process for building relationships with people who have the power to take your venture to the next level. The final part of chapter 13 coaches you through the elements of closing when an investor says yes.

Part One

CREATE YOUR PITCH

What if you could take everything world-changing about your venture and boil it down to a handful of words and images—a bundle of "ahas"—that you could pass along to people who could help you take your venture to the next level?

1

The Birth of the Pitch Deck

- What is a pitch deck?

- A short history of startup funding

- The pitch deck as your first prototype

What Is a Pitch Deck?

A pitch deck is a series of words and images that illustrate a venture's story and business model.

Pitch decks do three things: they get people to understand, they get people to care, and they get people to take action.

Entrepreneurs have used them to raise money, recruit employees, and close customers, partners, and suppliers. They are one of the most powerful tools early-stage entrepreneurs have at their disposal. They represent everything that is valuable about the startup—the vision, the team behind that vision, the core elements of its business model, and the insights into the customer that the venture plans to take advantage of and the industry that the venture hopes to disrupt.

There are two kinds of pitch decks:

1. **Presentation deck.** A visual to assist your oral presentation in an investor meeting or on stage at a demo day.

2. **Reading deck.** A more thorough and detailed deck that can be read and understood without you there.

A Short History of Startup Funding

If you were an entrepreneur in the 1960s, your options for funding were slim. Today, the startup landscape is overflowing with options.

It's not just in tech and health care. In 2014, $24.1 billion were invested into 73,400 ventures in angel investment alone. Add another $48.3 billion in 4,356 deals from venture capital. Then, double that from friends' and families' investments. Simultaneously, crowdfunding sites like Kickstarter and Indiegogo have opened the door for entirely new ways for entrepreneurs to fund and validate a business. With the passing of Title IV of the JOBS Act in 2012, almost anyone will be able to invest and receive equity in startups, not just the ultra-wealthy among us. We have moved from a few venture capital firms investing a few million dollars in startups to an almost infinite variety of funding sources collectively investing big-time money. The funding that many visionaries and entrepreneurs need is more available than it has ever been. You probably already know all this.

You also probably know something else: getting funded is hard. Depending on whom you talk to, it's either way too hard or not nearly hard enough.

You can guess what an entrepreneur would say. Entrepreneurs hate being held back. For a founder struggling to get funded, the problem is that there isn't nearly enough money to go around. Investors, on the other hand, hate losing money. Yet, they know that most of the startups they invest in will fail. For them, there aren't nearly enough good startups to go around.

Both sides agree that there needs to be a better way for the startups that have the best chance of success to get in front of the right kind of funding. To get there, entrepreneurs and investors look for ways to date each other—opportunities to charm or size up those on the other side of the table. Often, though not always, this means entrepreneurs spend their time wooing the investor while the investor plays the role of coy mistress, oscillating between flirtation and outright rejection.

The Age of the Business Plan

For years, the de facto entrée into this dating game was the business plan.

Originating with companies like DuPont and GM that had large government contracts with the US Department of Defense during World War II, the business plan takes cues from strategic planning within the US military. After an exhaustively thorough analysis of the industry, the competitive landscape, and target and potential markets, aspiring entrepreneurs would create a play-by-play of the business from launch to exit, articulating every detail of the marketing and operations plans, year-by-year growth in revenue and costs, and, ultimately, the amount they expect the market to value the company when they sell it or take it public.

This "business in sixty pages or less" gave entrepreneurs everything they needed to execute the venture. All that was left was for the right investor to come along, see the value of the plan, and pour a ton of cash into it. The idea caught full steam in the 1980s when every business professor, consultant, and professional coach in the nation published books to get the everyday Joe to become the next Steve Jobs or Bill Gates through one simple tool: the business plan. Sounds great, right?

Business plans for startups turn out to be one of those great ideas that fall apart in real life. Serial entrepreneur and Stanford professor Steve Blank puts it this way, "No business plan survives first contact with a customer." Plans work fine when all the information you need is available and all you have to do is execute. By definition, though, a startup exists in an environment of extreme uncertainty. A startup, as Steve Blank puts it, is an organization in search of a business model, not an organization with a plan to execute. Between 1982 and 1989, in the middle of the business plan craze, 79 percent of the companies in the *Inc.* 500 were launched without a formal business plan (including Apple and Microsoft). A more recent study found the same conclusion: business plans aren't critical to a startup's success.

Over the last ten years, and with the encouragement of books like Eric Ries's *The Lean Startup*, more and more entrepreneurs are abandoning the business plan as an opportunity analysis and launch tool in favor of tools that give them the flexibility to test and iterate the critical assumptions of their business model—assumptions like the problem you are solving, the cost of acquiring a single customer, and your defense against competition.

The Rise of the Pitch Deck

Entrepreneurs weren't the only ones to realize the business plan didn't work. With the explosion of venture capital starting in the 1970s, the investment banking industry found itself faced with ever-increasing stacks of potential deals. Tossing the business plan, it began to adopt new methods to quickly screen and pitch the opportunities before it. By using new presentation software like PowerPoint, investment bankers could replace the business plan with a series of slides that displayed big ideas, data, and other visuals while they gave a short pitch for the venture.

These presentations became known as "pitch decks." In addition to being shorter, this new way of presenting the business had several other key benefits. Pitch decks could be easily revised and customized, for example. A business plan took months to draft and redraft, but with a pitch deck, you could swap out individual slides for others and rework your entire presentation in a few minutes. You could also create a readable version of the presentation with the script written down on the slides so it could be printed out and sent to an investor ahead of time. Investors loved the new format, using the short presentations to filter out the obviously unqualified prospects and clue them in to opportunities where they could do a more thorough process of due diligence.

Perhaps the greatest advantage of a pitch deck was that it allowed the presenter to tell a great story. Investment bankers, like all great salespeople, knew that the data they had on a company wasn't nearly as important as their ability to tell a compelling story about that company. Like a filmmaker crafting the arc of a great movie, investment bankers made their living telling stories of how awesome the world would be if ACME Corp. bought AJAX Corp. to make the super-company ACMAJAX (the marketing department would sort out the naming). Pitch decks became the medium to tell that story. By the time Loomis entered the "Analyst Class of 2004" at a bulge bracket investment bank on Wall Street, his company devoted nearly a month of its three-month employee training program to PowerPoint. (You read that right.)

The next year, a serial entrepreneur named Paul Graham launched a three-month summer camp for startups. In it, very-early-stage startups would get access to mentoring, connections, and a small amount of seed money. The focus of the program, which Graham named Y Combinator, would be what he called "Demo Day," an all-day event where each team pitches its startup to a room of investors using a short presentation and a slide deck. As for business plans, "Not for us," the company writes on its site's FAQ. "We love demos, but we never read business plans." By 2011, that summer camp had become the "tech world's most prestigious program for budding digital entrepreneurs," according to *Wired* magazine. By then, it represented just one of as many as 200 startup accelerators in the United States.

That same year, the *Wall Street Journal* posed a question to a forum of startup mentors: **"Where do founders go wrong with business plans?" The short answer: when they make one.** The response from one of the mentors was to say, "Burn your business plan—before it burns you." Instead, the mentors said, focus on two things: your business model and your pitch. In another response titled, "Your Business Plan Isn't a Fundraising Tool Anymore," venture capitalist Paul Lee writes: "The best pitches come with a 10–12 slide PowerPoint that succinctly explains the business, with a link to the working service or website and the entrepreneurs biography/past experience. That's it."

Despite the cries from a remnant of business professors, consultants, and bank officers, the business plan was dead. In the world of startups, a new kind of tool had been born.

The Pitch Deck as Your First Prototype

You're at work, doing what you do every day, when, all of a sudden, this brilliant idea pops into your head.

"What if I . . . ?" or "Why isn't there a . . . ?" or "Wouldn't the world be so much better if . . . ?" That seed, once planted, grows so invasively that it's impossible to ignore and you can't help but do something about it.

Now, that first moment of insight might be totally wrong (it usually is). But what is most certainly not wrong is the questioning—that burning, impossible to ignore "why?" The hidden power of the pitch deck is its ability to infect others with the "why?"

Think about the excitement you feel about your venture. You probably can't help but tell people about it. There's a good chance your husband or wife is jealous. Let's be honest; you are obsessed. In another time period, you wouldn't be an entrepreneur; you'd be a crazy person. That's the kind of excitement you want others to feel when you pitch them. But getting others that excited about your idea will be maddeningly difficult if you don't know how to communicate it.

Getting Clarity on Your Idea

Too often, people passionate about ideas have articulated them across scraps of paper, e-mails, and thoughts in their head. This constellation of notes looks a lot like the way the idea looks in your brain: thousands of neurons firing thoughts, making connections through synapses in a web of what were once disconnected memories and inputs. But if you want someone else to understand that mess of a web, you've got to find a way to get it into something more accessible.

Committing a business model to paper is the first step to making the model better. It forces the entrepreneur to break down the business into each of its components and to articulate those components clearly. You might say you can't make a business model better until you actually have the business model written down.

For first-time founders, advice on their idea is more valuable than money and is likely to be a precursor to it. There's an old cliché we heard often while interviewing investors and entrepreneurs for this book: **If you want advice for your startup, ask for money. If you want money, ask for advice. To succeed, you will need both.**

You owe it to yourself and anyone you meet with to have a description of the vision and business model of the venture ready to send in advance. This artifact then becomes something others can react to, comment on, and add or subtract from. There is no faster or cheaper way to iterate your venture when it is in its earliest stages than to create and revise a pitch deck. For many pre-seed-stage startups, the pitch deck literally is the startup, the very first prototype. It articulates the critical assumptions of your venture, and almost more importantly, it gives you a chance to practice telling others why they should care about it.

So how do you create a pitch deck for your venture? The basic anatomy of a pitch deck is surprisingly simple. It aligns with the critical questions investors ask themselves when looking at a potential opportunity. We introduce you to them next.

2

The Building Blocks of a Pitch Deck

The building blocks of a pitch deck are the slides. Slides are like the panels of a comic strip; they break down the story of your venture into discrete digestible chunks. Each slide highlights a different aspect of the venture and furthers the plot of the pitch. Eventually, you'll have a whole archive of slides to draw from and sequence for each meeting or presentation. These are the essential ten (not including your cover page):

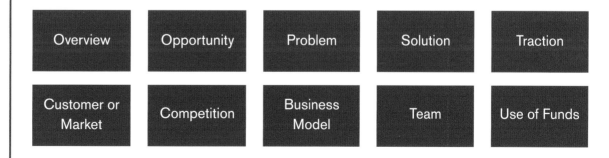

Cover
What should I expect?

Skycatch

Karma

Able

What is it?

The cover slide captures the audience's attention, sets the tone for the pitch, and serves as "white space" during a presentation so you can express gratitude for your audience's time, show your passion for your venture, and build trust by mentioning mutual connections.

What should I demonstrate?

- **Clean logo.** Your logo is the face of your brand; it can be very important to your overall image.

- **Inviting picture.** You might include an engaging picture of your product or customer.

- **Descriptive title.** Put "Investor Briefing" or "Investor Presentation" somewhere on the front cover with the date. Dates help you keep track of different versions.

What questions do I need to answer?

- Does the cover make you want to open the pitch deck?

- Does the cover visual communicate what the product is or who it serves?

Overview
Who are we?

Contactually is a **relationship marketing platform** that helps professionals keep and generate business from their existing network.

Contactually

Karma

Reaction, Inc.

What is it?

The company overview is your "elevator pitch"—the fifteen-second version of your deck. It describes a problem you see in the world and how you are going to solve it. Give your audience a small taste of what your company does, but leave them hungry for more.

What should I demonstrate?

- **Clarity.** It should be extremely easy to understand what the company does.

- **Swagger.** Startups are bold, audacious undertakings. Your summary of the venture should demonstrate that you have the energy and the confidence to take on something big.

- **Passion.** If you don't care about what you're doing, no one else will.

What questions do I need to answer?

- What exactly does your company do?

- What industry are you in?

- Is this a novel idea?

The Elevator Pitch

An elevator pitch is the simplest, quickest way to describe what your venture is and what makes it so amazing. It's the pitch you prepare for when you only have fifteen seconds to catch someone's attention—like when you meet him in an elevator or see him on a street waiting for an Uber or Lyft ride.

The great screenwriter Blake Snyder argued that the secret to all great pitches is learning to combine the familiar with the intriguing. You must start with something your audience knows well. Then, surprise them with an ironic twist that captures their interest and will make them want to know more.

Use an analogy. Do not assume your audience knows what you are talking about. Describe your venture with common language and universal images that appeal to your prospective investor and future customers.

Don't talk about what your product does; talk about what it does for your customer. This is a really common mistake for engineer types. The classic maxim from Harvard professor Ted Levitt illustrates the idea well: "People buy a ¼" drill bit not because they want a ¼" drill bit, but because they want a ¼" hole."

Pick a fight. Don't be afraid to build off of a universally hated experience. Picking a fight can be a clear sign that you're solving a real problem.

Tell your vision. Don't get lost in describing the product. Describe the new and better world you want your product to help create.

Examples

The first [what you are] that doesn't suck.

- **SilverCar:** The first car rental company that doesn't suck.

- **Karma:** The first mobile provider that doesn't suck.

The [easiest/fastest/funnest/best] way to [your solution].

- **Shyp:** The easiest way to ship your stuff.

It's [analogy] for [your space].

- **TreeHouse:** It's Whole Foods for Home Depot.

We help [your customer] do [your solution] by [your product]. Or, We are a [your product] that helps [your customer] do [your solution].

- **Contactually:** Contactually is a relationship marketing platform that helps professionals keep and generate business from their existing networks.

Opportunity

What's happening in this market?
Why now?

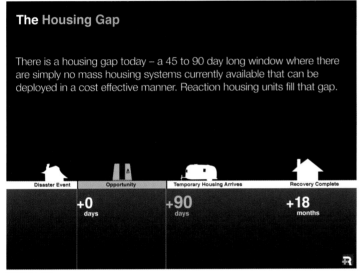

The Housing Gap

There is a housing gap today – a 45 to 90 day long window where there are simply no mass housing systems currently available that can be deployed in a cost effective manner. Reaction housing units fill that gap.

| Disaster Event | Opportunity | Temporary Housing Arrives | Recovery Complete |
| +0 days | | +90 days | +18 months |

Reaction, Inc.

SOLS Systems

GROWTH IN AERIAL DATA MARKET

Skycatch

What is it?

The opportunity slide is your chance to describe your industry and how your business will work within it. You will describe trends within that environment, the size of your market, and the growth potential of your venture.

The opportunity slide is the 40,000-foot picture of your product's space. You want the investors to see the trends and market conditions that will give you an entrance into the market and a competitive position. If your audience agrees with you on how things actually are right now, they will be open to the particular problems and solution you describe.

What should I demonstrate?

- **Explosive market sectors.** By explosive, we mean growing very, very fast. The faster your market is growing, the bigger the opportunity for your venture will be.

- **Confusion and ambiguity in the market.** A lack of clarity allows ventures to easily differentiate themselves from others.

- **Thoroughness.** This slide is proof that you have done some serious research and really understand the market better than your audience does.

What questions do I need to answer?

- What trends is your company riding?

- How big is the market?

- How big can your company be?

- What are the macro- and micro-trends that your company will be riding?

Problem

What are you trying to solve?

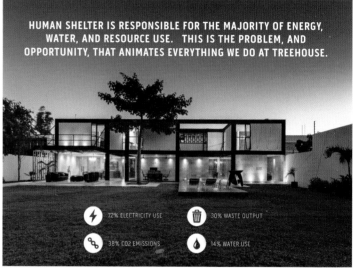

HUMAN SHELTER IS RESPONSIBLE FOR THE MAJORITY OF ENERGY, WATER, AND RESOURCE USE. THIS IS THE PROBLEM, AND OPPORTUNITY, THAT ANIMATES EVERYTHING WE DO AT TREEHOUSE.

72% ELECTRICITY USE   30% WASTE OUTPUT

38% CO2 EMISSIONS   14% WATER USE

TreeHouse

First Opinion

Hinge

What is it?

Entrepreneurship, at its core, is about solving problems. The bigger the problem, the better.

In your problem slide, describe the problem you are solving and how and why that problem is painful. Your audience should feel as if an injustice has been done. In a meeting, you'll know if your problem hits home when the investors begin nodding their heads in agreement. Describe the problem at a high level first and then quickly transition to a specific story of a customer to make the problem personal. People don't empathize with big, general problems; they empathize with the struggles of specific people with names and faces.

Not all companies solve new problems; some focus on solving age-old problems in a way that changes customer preferences. This is especially true in apparel, restaurants, and many consumer product goods. If you have one of these ventures, you should focus on the opportunity before you (the previous slide) rather than the problem you are trying to solve.

What should I demonstrate?

- **A big problem in a big market.** Provide a very large and specific number of people who feel the pain of this problem every day.

- **Deep understanding.** Confidently and empathetically display how well you understand the complex market dynamics surrounding the problem.

- **A specific person.** Consider presenting the problem by telling a short story of a real person and how he experiences the problem.

What questions do I need to answer?

- What is the problem?

- How big is the problem?

- Why does the problem exist?

- How is the problem currently being addressed?

Solution

What are you doing about it?

Connect

Hinge

Tegu

What is it?

By this point, you and your audience agree on what is happening in the industry and you have introduced a huge problem. Now, it is time to pull out all the stops. Show them your magic, your one-of-a-kind solution to the problem. You want the investors to marvel at it. You can also remind them how you can defend what you are doing through intellectual property claims. Develop use cases to demonstrate how your customer will be delighted with your solution.

Make your solution as realistic and interactive as possible. In meetings, bring the physical product or do an interactive demonstration. Short (one- to three-minute) videos, illustrations, screenshots, pictures, prototypes, samples, sketches, or demos are all great ways to show rather than tell your solution.

If you learn nothing from this book, remember this: never use bullet points for your solution slide!

What should I demonstrate?

- **Beauty.** There should be an element of elegance to your solution. It should feel like the way things *should* be.

- **Surprise.** Your solution should feel like nothing your audience has ever seen.

- **Repeatable and scalable.** It should be evident in your solution that what you are building can be replicated across the market.

- **Solving something painful.** It should be clear that your solution relieves a persistant pain point the customer currently experiences.

- **Team excellence.** This is your chance to brag and show off that you have an awesome team that has built something that delights.

What questions do I need to answer?

- Does it solve the customer's problems like magic?

- Is the customer going to crave this product?

- What will the customer's life be like once the problem is solved?

- How are you going to pull this off?

- Is it awesome?

Traction

What evidence do you have that shows this will be successful?

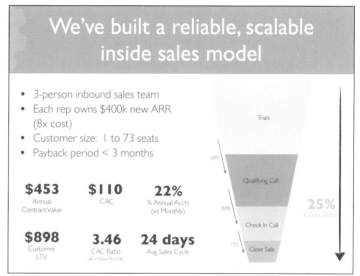

Contactually

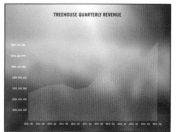

TreeHouse

Beacon

What is it?

The goal of this slide is to demonstrate that each of your assumptions about the venture is proving true and you are making significant progress. The most common way to show traction is through growing sales or users—one with the "hockey-stick" graph—but you can also focus on other key metrics you have identified. Investors don't want to feel that a venture needs them. Traction helps convince an investor that the idea is going to be a success no matter what. If you are preproduct and don't have any meaningful milestones or metrics to display, you can use this slide as an opportunity to illustrate your sales and marketing strategy.

What should I demonstrate?

- A pattern of fast-growing momentum.

- Clarity around what you are measuring and why it matters.

- A clear sales process you use to attract, educate, qualify, close, and provide after-sale service for your customers.

What questions do I need to answer?

- Is there massive growth?

- Where are the venture's assumptions proving true?

- What is the strategy to reach and close more customers?

Customer or Market

Who are your customers—and how many of them are out there?

Reaction, Inc.

Contactually

SOLS Systems

What is it?

In this slide, you demonstrate how well you know your customers and the market they represent. Describe where they live, what they like to do, and how much they'd be willing to spend. If you already have sales, you can use those as an example. Also describe the market, that is, how many potential customers are out there who will want to buy your product.

What should I demonstrate?

- **The customer.** Describe the person in a way that reminds listeners of someone they know.

- **A clearly defined market.** Give specific numbers for how many people fit your customer descriptions. Include how many people might possibly buy your product, what percentage of those people you expect to buy it, and which ones you will target first.

- **Revenue.** It's much easier to argue that there's a demand for your product if you have paying customers.

What questions do I need to answer?

- Who is your customer(s)?

- How will you reach the customer?

- What is the acquisition cost per customer?

- Is your customer willing to pay for your product or service?

Market Sizing

Market sizing is about answering a few key questions on who your customers are, how they are segmented, and how big the opportunity they represent is. The science of market sizing is finding hard data on your customers—how many there are, the amount of revenue you could get from each customer, and the percentage of the market you hope to capture. The art of market sizing is deciding what key characteristics differentiate your customers from everyone else in the world in order to make those calculations. For ventures that are targeting new markets or helping to create one, the challenge of market sizing becomes even harder. You can simplify the process by focusing on those key questions that hide behind the terms many investors use.

Total addressable market: How big can this get?

The total addressable market (TAM) is about figuring out how many people could possibly buy your product, how much revenue you could make from each one, and the product of those two numbers. Many ventures find TAM by searching industry profiles from big research companies like Gartner, Forrester, Dun & Bradstreet, and Hoover's for big, sweeping, industrywide categories like "e-commerce" and use whatever number they give for that industry. A more reliable way to find TAM is to pick one to two relevant characteristics (that is, "e-commerce businesses in America") and multiply the number of people or businesses with those characteristics by your expected lifetime value of a single customer.

Served addressable market: Who do you plan to serve—and how big an opportunity is that?

The served addressable market (SAM) is a smaller collection of potential customers who you are actively choosing to serve. With SAM, you are increasing your degree of resolution into who your customers are by choosing one to two more characteristics, like location or product, and filtering your bigger TAM with them. The process for calculating SAM is the same as TAM: choose your filters, count the number of people who match those filters, and multiply by your expected lifetime value of a single customer.

Beachhead market: Who are you selling to first?

Your beachhead market is the first market you will sell to. These customers should all have a similar job they need done that they could hire your product to do. To find these customers, you have to find special characteristics that only your customers have. These characteristics are unlikely to be traditional ones like location, industry, or income level. Harvard professor Clayton Christensen describes a fast-food restaurant that was trying to improve its milkshake sales. When traditional segments like demographics failed, it started looking at the "job" that people were hiring a milkshake to do. When it dug in, the company found that most people bought milkshakes either to entertain themselves during a long morning commute or to treat a son or daughter in the afternoon. This insight helped it improve its product and gave it specific filters for segmenting its customers (that is, those with long morning commutes or parents with small children). For your beachhead, choose a job that people hire your product to do, find a measurable characteristic that unites those people, count them up, and multiply them by your expected lifetime customer value.

Competition

Who or what will steal your customers?

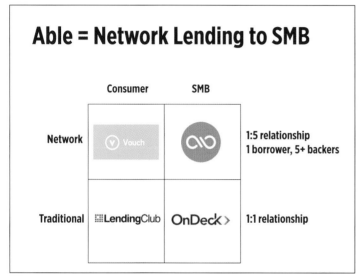

Able

Reaction, Inc.

Contactually

What is it?

Every venture has competition. *Every* venture.

Your customers must be doing something right now to cope with the problem you solve. That "something" is your competitor.

List competitors and describe how each competes in the market. Then, show what differentiates you from competitors and what advantage you have over them. Partnerships, technology expertise, intellectual property, simplicity, business processes, and networks can all be significant advantages. Many founders find it helpful to create a map of the competitive landscape, using important aspects of the product as x and y axes. For example, if you have a product that is both priced affordably and is a great value, you could put "cost" on the x axis and "value" on the y axis and place your product in the top-left quadrant (high value, low cost), with the rest of your competitors spread throughout the other quadrants. By doing this, you visually demonstrate how your product differentiates itself from other players in the market.

What should I demonstrate?

- **Industry knowledge.** You should know your competitors and their unique advantages and disadvantages.

- **Sober judgment.** Entrepreneurs caught up in the brilliance of their own ideas might miss major warning signs. An investor wants to know whether or not you are underestimating the threat of competition.

- **Differentiation.** Is it clear that you are different enough to compete?

- **Unique advantage.** What is your specific advantage over your competitors?

What questions do I need to answer?

- Who are your primary and secondary competitors and in what ways do they compete for your customers?

- Are there any unknown or potential competitors that would have a better advantage than you if they entered the market?

- Do you displace commonly used companies?

- How will you disrupt the current competitive landscape?

- Are you faster, cheaper, better?

- Why won't an incumbent rip your product off and roll it out faster than you can?

Business Model
How will you make money?

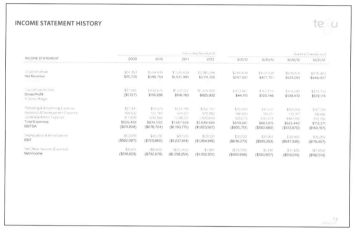

Tegu

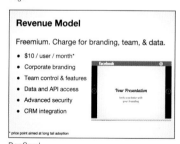

DocSend

Beacon

What is it?

Don't worry; showing how the business makes money is much simpler than you think.

For example, a solid financial model will answer the following questions:

1. How much does it cost to acquire a customer?

2. How much cash will you make from that customer, over the course of their lifetime with you?

3. How do your costs break down, per unit and on a monthly basis?

Prerevenue companies may have the good fortune of making up assumptions and financials, but that is not an excuse for having unrealistic projections. Since the pitch deck is designed to introduce the idea, it's not too important to show a full-blown financial model with every assumption, sensitivity, and margin analysis. However, it should include the important aspects such as revenue, gross profit, earnings before interest, taxes, depreciation, and amortization (EBITDA), net income, burn rate, and cash flow. Equally as important is to contextualize your math (as in, "if we get 1 percent of the market, then we will have hit our revenue projection").

What should I demonstrate?

- **Consistency.** There should be a clear relationship between how costs and revenues grow over time.

- **Financial literacy.** You know how to think about the financials of a startup.

- **Level-headedness.** You are not overly optimistic about your projections or too cautious.

What questions do I need to answer?

- Can you acquire customers for less than a third of their lifetime value?

- What is your monthly burn rate—how much money are you spending a month?

- Are the revenue projections reasonable?

- Are costs legitimate?

How Financial Models Work

Assumptions → [create] →   **Projections** → [that give you] → **Critical Insights**

All financial models begin with assumptions—a series of guesses about when a business will gain customers, how many customers it will gain, and how that growth will affect costs and, ultimately, profit.

Common assumptions:

- **Customer acquisition cost.** How much does it cost to acquire one customer?

- **Revenue growth.** How fast do you expect revenue to grow? By how many customers a month? By what percentage a month?

Those assumptions, played out over time, create projections for the venture's future financial health. A full financial model will have three projections:

- **Income statement.** How much money the business brought in through sales, the cost of making and selling the product, and the amount of money left over (net income).

- **Cash flow statement.** How much cash a business has in the bank. With complex businesses that have things like inventory or debt, a cash flow statement can be very different from its income statement.

- **Balance sheet.** A list of a venture's assets—things like cash, buildings, and inventory—balanced against its liabilities—things like debt—and all the owners' equity stakes.

The reason you create a financial model is to gain a few critical insights about the venture that can tell you how risky or attractive the opportunity is:

- **Cash flow.** Will it make money? When?

- **Burn rate.** How much cash are you losing each month?

- **Profit margin.** Your net income divided by revenues.

- **Breakeven.** When will the venture turn cash flow positive?

- **Pricing.** Do small decreases in pricing eat up your profit margin and cause you to run out of cash?

Team
Who is going to pull this off?

First Opinion

Hinge

Shift

What is it?

In the team slide, you want to give the background for each of the key team members, including their current roles, prior experience, significant accomplishments, and education. If there are any major investors or advisers, you can name them here. Keep your bio to less than a minute total when presenting. Your goals are to build rapport, be known, and build confidence that the team can accomplish the mission.

What should I demonstrate?

- **Brevity.** Each bio should be only seventy-five words or less.*

- **Domain expertise.** You have the experience and insight to get the job done.

- **Passion, intensity, and a good team culture.** You know the kind of team culture you are creating and that each person is committed to it.

*You should also prepare a longer (250–500 word) bio, in case an investor asks for it. The point of the pitch deck bio is to get your audience's attention, not tell your life story.

What questions do I need to answer?

- Why are you the right people for the job?

- Is this team sufficient to accomplish the goal?

- Are there others who need to be hired?

Use of Funds
What do you want and why?

We're raising a $5M Series A with three goals

1. **Ramp up sales**: Scale inside sales team and develop outbound sales practice

2. **Optimize the platform for scale & ROI**: Improve performance & deliver value, esp for teams

3. **Emphasize thought leadership**: Drive lead gen via content marketing and partnerships

Contactually

First Opinion

Reaction, Inc.

What is it?

A good pitch deck has a clear ask of the investor. This is married with an understanding of what the investor gets in return and what the money will be used for. Some entrepreneurs like to create a slide with every way the company can be sold, potential acquisition targets, initial public offerings, yada yada. Everyone will tell you something different, but we think it's best to focus on your company. Spell out how you actually plan to use the money you are asking for. What will it give you in terms of resources or achieved milestones?

What should I demonstrate?

- **Clarity.** You specifically and clearly state what the funds will be used for.

- **Milestones.** You should show what you expect to achieve by the time the money is gone.

What questions do I need to answer?

- What size and type of investment are you looking for?

- How will you spend it?

- What will you accomplish with it?

- Who else is likely to be participating in this investment round?

Extra Slides

Although the ten building blocks make up the core of most decks, there are an almost infinite number of slides you might add, depending on your venture and the way you tell your story. Here's a list of forty-one other slides to build into your deck or add to an appendix.

1. **Frequently asked questions (FAQs).** Usually, there are about five to ten questions that almost everyone asks. Build trust with investors by facing the difficult questions head on. Create a slide and put the questions and answers next to each other.

2. **History.** Context can be helpful. A history slide, typically laid out as a timeline, gives you the ability to show your company's key mile markers, for example, incorporation, team formed, first product sold, money raised, and record sales month.

3. **Products.** Simply show your product(s). Make the product the hero of the slide: large, front and center, with little or no text around it.

4. **Market.** The market slide can show anything you want about the market you operate in. Characteristics like where the market is heading, how large it is, the changes taking place are important to lay out.

5. **Patents.** Patents can add value to your company. If you have them, show them. Patents are a clear demonstration that you can defend your venture from copycats.

6. **People you are learning from.** Few entrepreneurs include this slide; it's one of our favorites. List everyone you are learning from: advisers, friends, investors, and so on. They can be people you know personally or whose work you follow and admire. The list shows you are curious and are sourcing a wide range of feedback from key people.

7. **Executive summary.** This simple overview of the venture and its opportunity usually consists of one or two sentences, placed in the middle of the slide.

8. **Income statement, balance sheet statement, and cash flow statement.** This trio makes up what people usually mean when they say "financials." The later the stage of the venture, the more important these elements become.

9. **Investment highlights.** List well-known and respected investors who have already invested in the business, as well as previous successful funding rounds.

10. **Milestones achieved.** This timeline of important achievements shows that your team knows how to get stuff done. If you haven't released your product yet, milestones are a great way to demonstrate momentum.

11. **Branding.** Consumer-facing and product-based startups often live and die by the experience they create for their customer. If the physical experience of your product matters, this slide gives you a chance to show that off.

12. **Product road map.** Investors want to know where you are headed next. What's most important in the next three, six, and twelve months? A product road map, usually displayed through a timeline or Gantt chart, gives your audience a full picture of the long-term vision of the product and your priorities.

13. **Mission.** A mission statement should be actionable and personal. It answers the question: Why do we exist? The mission statement should help your team make better decisions and gives others insight into what's driving the venture.

14. **Vision.** Vision statements are aspirational; they describe the kind of world you are striving to create. The goal of this slide is to get others to buy into your vision of the future.

15. **Pictures.** This really isn't a slide type, but a storytelling technique. Using a picture with few or no

words can help immerse your audience into a scene or experience that you want them to understand.

16. **Supply chain.** This diagram traces where and how you source your raw materials and inputs for your product. A solid and protected supply chain can be a hedge against competition and an unfair advantage over existing players or new entrants.

17. **How it works.** Quickly explain to your audience how your product does what you say it does.

18. **Risks.** This slide lists the biggest challenges you face as a venture. Examples of risks include assumptions you've made that you have to prove or industry dynamics that make you vulnerable. This slide explains that you understand exactly what those risks are and what you are doing to defend against them.

19. **Differentiation.** If you are in what others may consider to be a crowded market, this slide explains what makes you different.

20. **Locations.** Show a current map of where your customers are or where your product is available.

21. **Geographic growth plans.** This future-oriented version of the "locations" slide shows where you plan to be over the next several months.

22. **Screenshots.** Screenshots of your product are a simple way to show your audience exactly what you are doing and lets them experience your product as a customer would.

23. **Sales funnel.** This diagram demonstrates how you are systematically getting customers. A typical funnel moves through a process of gathering leads, qualifying those leads, educating potential customers and answering objections, closing, and then following up with after-sales service. Investors like to know how you are moving people through each stage in the process and what the conversion rates are from one stage to the next.

24. **Customer acquisition strategy.** This slide is a different way of showing the same thing as the sales funnel: how you plan to get customers. Be specific on this slide. E-mail marketing campaigns, Google AdWords and Facebook ads, influencer or ambassador programs, referral programs, trade shows, and cold-pitching are all examples of potential acquisition strategies. In addition to showing the strategy, give data on the expected costs and conversion rates of these strategies.

25. **Customer lifetime value.** How much will each customer be worth over the course of his or her engagement with your product? Show this number and how

you arrived at it (how many times do they purchase over what period of time?).

26. **Designs/blueprints.** Similar to the "how it works" slide, this gives you a chance to demonstrate the underlying mechanics of a product.

27. **History and background.** Tell the backstory of your team and the venture that led to where you are today. This slide can help you demonstrate expertise and previous success in your space.

28. **Unique value proposition.** Popularized by tools like the Business Model Canvas and Lean Canvas, this slide presents a clear statement of what makes you different and why customers will buy your product.

29. **Competitive or unfair advantage.** What difficult-to-copy advantage do you have over competitors?

30. **Pipeline.** Depending on the size of each deal, this list of the customers that you are currently negotiating with shows the names and logos of well-known customers or calculates the total size of those deals in dollars to show likely future sales.

31. **Strategic partnerships.** This slide shows the names or logos of strategic partnerships that will help you get more customers, lower costs, or break into new markets.

32. **Customer quotes.** Customer quotes give others a more intimate picture of why people buy your product or service.

33. **Comparable companies.** This slide lists the companies in your space and key metrics.

34. **Go-to-market strategy.** Which customers do you plan to target first and how do you plan to target them? Include evidence for why this is the right first move to make.

35. **Case study.** Tell a story of a specific customer or partnership and how your product did amazing things for them.

36. **Organization chart.** This slide is a diagram of your current team, their titles, and who reports to whom. Show a typical organization chart in a hierarchical tree format.

37. **Exit strategy.** Explain your strategy for whether you plan to exit the business through acquisition, IPO, or something else, when you plan to exit. For acquisition exit strategy, include a list of potential acquirers.

38. **Exits.** List the companies that are similar to yours and have had successful exits. Include their valuations at the time of the exit.

39. **Conclusion.** This is the "sum it all up" slide—a clear statement that explains the power of your venture and the opportunity your audience has to be a part of it.

40. **Technology.** Describe and visualize the core technology that powers your product and keeps your venture from being copied by others.

41. **Valuation.** List the terms of the deal you are offering: how much you are raising and the valuation of the company. If you are structuring your raise with a convertible note, include the valuation cap and the discount you are offering.

Beyond Just Slides: Story, Design, and Text

In "The Building Blocks of a Pitch Deck," we gave you a basic outline. Most entrepreneurs stop there. But over the next three chapters, we're going to dig into the key elements that transform a deck from a lifeless document that fails to inspire into one of your biggest assets: story, design, and text. For perspective, you might spend 25 percent of your time on the architecture and the remaining 75 percent on these components that really differentiate your deck.

3

Story

Stories explain, captivate, disturb, and inspire. They can tell us there is something very, very wrong, and they can give us a vision for what we never thought possible. Great stories are about what's true inside all of us. That's what makes them work. Entrepreneurship is about telling a story that connects the deep needs of a group of people with a repeatable solution. For your deck, stories are the fabric that stitches everything together. You will use stories in three primary ways:

1. To create a narrative arc that ties your slide deck together.

2. To explain one or more of your slides.

3. To have as a reservoir of things to discuss and ways to respond to questions during a conversation.

Whether you're presenting in person or sending the deck for someone to read, without the elements of story, your deck is just a bunch of boring slides.

In this section, we outline four basic story archetypes and use the case study of Scott Harrison, founder and CEO of charity: water, to illustrate their power. In the last decade, charity: water has revolutionized the nonprofit industry, put a significant dent in the global water crisis, and set the standard for raising money in the twenty-first century for any venture.

Its efforts have funded more than 16,000 water projects and brought clean water to 5.2 million people in 25 countries. It has also raised over $185 million from 1 million supporters.

As a nonprofit, charity: water's engine works a bit differently than a typical startup, but the basic stories it uses to sell others on its vision are universal to any venture.

Key Elements:

- The origin story
- The customer story
- The industry story
- The venture growth story

The Origin Story

After eighteen years in a loving, conservative family, Scott Harrison decided it was time to rebel. Like a kid in a bad teen movie, he moved to New York, joined a band, and started drinking. The band broke up immediately, but he discovered you could make a lot more money booking shows than playing them. If you got good, companies would pay you to be seen drinking their booze at a party. That began Scott's life as a nightclub promoter. Every night, he would convince people to buy $20 bottles of champagne for $200. Budweiser paid him $2,000 a month to drink its beer; Bacardi paid him another $2,000 to drink its rum.

Ten years later on a New Year's trip to Uruguay, he realized he was the worst person he knew. Surrounded by beautiful people and Dom Pérignon magnums, he said to himself, "I'm never going to find what I'm looking for where I'm looking for it." Hung over the next day, he started reading the Bible. He came across this verse: "True religion is to look after widows and orphans in their distress and to keep oneself from being polluted." Not the most encouraging verse for a guy who got people wasted for a living.

He knew he had to do something big. Making a deal with God, he decided to spend a year serving the poor to make up for the ten he'd wasted. Eventually, an organization agreed to take him on as a volunteer photographer if he paid them $500 a month. "Here's my credit card," he said. "Where are we going?"

Liberia. Doctors from the organization Mercy Ships traveled from country to country, giving operations to help people with facial deformities. Overwhelmed by the poverty and sickness surrounding him, Scott broke down. He photographed thousands of people—people with tumors on their lips so large that they were suffocating or whose communities shunned them and threw rocks at them—all of which were healed by simple surgeries. The first year went by. Scott signed up for another. In the second year, he discovered one of the things that made people sick: dirty water. Standing in front of a beautiful still pond on the outside of a village, he watched as a young girl dipped her bucket into the green water and pulled it out to drink. "No wonder there are things growing on people faces; look at what they're drinking," he thought.

He moved back to New York City, unable to get that image of the girl drinking from a swamp out of his mind. Eight hundred million people just like her lacked access to clean water every day. So, at the age of thirty and $30,000 in debt, he moved onto a friend's couch and started charity: water with the goal of ending the water crisis in his lifetime.

Seven years later, every time Scott speaks about charity: water, he opens with that story.

Images copyright Scott Harrison

Your Origin Story

The journey from loving home to the nightclubs of New York to the poorest parts of the world is Scott's origin story—his personal "why." It's how he came to discover his mission and start pursuing it, and it is at the core of his ability to rally people to his cause.

If you want to get people fired up about an idea, they need to know why you are fired up about that idea. Scott knows that sharing the story of how he started keeps people from seeing charity: water as just another charity and creates a bond between him and his audience. "Many people want to know what is driving the entrepreneur forward, and learn more about his or her character before they invest," Scott said. "I think one of the most important

Diagram of Joseph Campbell's Hero's Journey

Gray circle = inner journey

Blue circle = outer journey (character transformation)

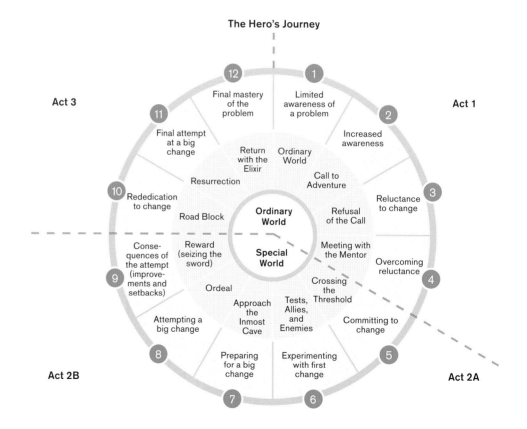

things is being able to tell your personal story in a way that engages people."

What has brought you to this moment? Why were you "made for a time such as this"? What has prepared you to take on this challenge? Why is it so important to you personally? Why would you do what you're doing for free? Like Scott, many of the best and most successful entrepreneurs have found a beautiful match between their personal passions and the companies they launch. They talk about their journey in a way that feels as if their ventures are the fulfillment of their life stories. The beautiful part is that it is true.

A founder's origin story follows the classic pattern known as the hero's journey, originally described by Joseph Campbell in *The Hero with a Thousand Faces*. It starts with the hero living life as usual, unaware of any great need or problem. Then, one day, he's faced with a deep and troubling experience that keeps him from ever living "life as usual" again. That experience leads to a new sense of purpose, causes him to take great and sometimes risky action, and ultimately changes the way he sees the world. All great hero stories follow this storyline—including those about entrepreneurs.

The Elements of an Origin Story

1. You're living life as normal, unaware of anything wrong with the world.

2. Suddenly, you have an epiphany and feel a call to adventure.

3. You accept the challenge and take bold action.

4. That action gives you a new sense of purpose and understanding that continues to motivate you today.

The Customer Story

Scott also tells another type of story whenever he speaks: the story about the people charity: water helps. He talks about a woman who walks eight hours a day for water, carrying a clay pot that weighs ten or fifteen pounds empty, and another thirty pounds when it is full. One day, she comes back into the village with her clay pot filled with water, and she slips and falls. The clay pot breaks. She takes the rope she used to wrap the pot around her back and uses it to hang herself on a tree in the middle of the village.

Or, he tells the story of a woman named Helen Appio. Helen grew up in a village in northern Uganda. Before her village had clean water, Helen woke up before dawn to walk nearly a mile and a half to the closest water point. There, she would wait for hours with hundreds of other women to fill her two five-gallon jerry cans. When she walked back to the village, she was forced to make a decision: How do I use these ten gallons of water today? Cook a meal with it?

Images copyright Esther Havens

Drink it? Clean the children's clothes? Then, charity: water built a well in her village. Now that she has water, everything is different. "I'm happy now," she says. "I have time to eat, my children can go to school, and I can even work in my garden, take a shower, and come back for more water if I want. I'm bathing so well."

Seeing her bright face and beautiful green dress, a woman from charity: water told her, "Well, you look great." Helen put her hands on the woman's shoulders. "Yes," she said. "Now, I am beautiful." Recounting that story, Scott marvels, "What an amazing thing. What a crazy thing! To be able to restore someone's dignity and make them feel beautiful, just by tripling the quantity of water."

A venture's success rests on its ability to make the lives of the people it serves better. By telling the story of a person your venture serves, you demonstrate how it solves a deep need in the world. By articulating your value proposition as it relates to a single, real-life person, founders can help the people they are trying to persuade understand the true potential of what they are working on.

These stories follow a very predictable pattern, as well. First, they introduce someone with a big and frustrating problem. They describe what life looks like for that person, how she tries to overcome or solve her problem now, and how nothing she tries works. Then they describe how, one day, that person came in contact with your product, which, almost miraculously, solved the problem she has been struggling with for so long. The stories end by describing what life is like for that person now that she has your product. She is happy. She can't help but tell others about it. She is free to do so many other things that before she only dreamed of.

These stories communicate the value of a venture in microcosm and give others an anchor to focus their attention.

The Elements of a Customer Story*

1. Meet Joe. Joe has a problem. This problem really bothers Joe.

2. Joe tried this and this, but no matter what he does he can't solve his problem.

3. Until, one day, Joe finds [your amazing product].

4. Now Joe is so happy, he tells all his friends. Don't you want to be like Joe?

*Adapted from Lee LeFever, *The Art of Explanation* (Hoboken, NJ: Wiley, 2013).

The Industry Story

Scott tells another story about the charitable industry itself. He talks about how, after coming back from Africa, he discovered his friends were disillusioned and suspicious of charities. With the image of charity directors buying BMWs and multimillion-dollar mansions with other people's donations stuck in their heads, no one was interested in giving. "How much money would actually reach the people? How will I know where my money is going?" they asked.

Scott realized that the charity industry was ripe for innovation. People didn't give because they thought too much money went to the operations of the charity itself. So, Scott opened two bank accounts when he launched charity: water: one for all the overhead of the business, which he would fund with money from private donors, and another for the work of the charity. This way, 100 percent of the funds he raised publicly would go directly to the people he served.

Another reason people didn't give was because they didn't feel connected to the impact their money was having. With most organizations, it felt like any money you gave went into a black hole. You never knew where it went or what kind of effect it had. Scott decided charity: water would make a commitment to never fund a project unless it could know it exists through photos and GPS coordinates.

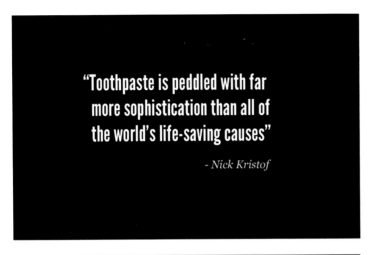

"Toothpaste is peddled with far more sophistication than all of the world's life-saving causes"

- *Nick Kristof*

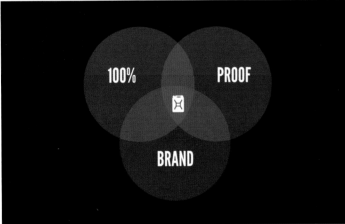

100%   PROOF

BRAND

Images copyright Scott Harrison

Whenever someone gave to charity: water, he or she would be able to go to a Google map and literally see the well that was built with his or her money.

Finally, he realized that charities were often phenomenal at the service they gave but horrible at raising money. The damning words of *New York Times* columnist Nicholas Kristof motivated him: "Toothpaste is peddled with far more sophistication than all of the world's life-saving causes." There were no effective charity brands. They had horrible websites, hosted speaking events that nobody came to, and were constantly limited by a lack of funds. To be successful, Scott decided, charity: water would create an amazing brand that people wanted to identify themselves with.

This is Scott's industry story: how, at a macrolevel, the trends and environment of the charitable industry created a unique opportunity for charity: water to do something amazing. In the pursuit of ending the water crisis, it would also reinvent charity.

Telling the industry story gives your audience the confidence that the larger forces at play around you are moving in your favor. The story also shows that you have a deep understanding of how your venture fits into the larger social, political, and economic picture. Can you identify the trends and signs of the space you are in? Who does well in good times? Who does well in bad times? What are the barriers to entry in your industry? What effects do customers, suppliers, substitute solutions, rivals, and the threat of new entrants have on you and other companies in the space?

Industry stories usually follow this kind of pattern: They start by describing where the industry is now and how it got there. They identify the key players in that industry, and the assumptions they make and problems they are facing. Then, they introduce a few key cultural, technological, or economic trends that present an opportunity for someone to do something different. These stories are proof that the wind is at your back and not in your face.

The Elements of an Industry Story

1. For a long time, the industry has operated according to a set of assumptions based on the environment it grew up within.

2. As a result of specific social, technological, or economic factors, those assumptions are no longer holding true, creating problems for the big players in the industry.

3. This change creates a unique opportunity for someone to step in and take advantage of these new circumstances.

The Venture Growth Story

The fourth story Scott tells is charity: water's growth story. This story illustrates how the other stories—his personal discovery of his mission, the transformation of the people he serves, and the emergence of an opportunity caused by broader societal forces—have come together to enable charity: water's amazing growth and impact.

Scott launched charity: water by doing the only thing he knew how to do: throw a party. Luring them with free booze, he convinced seven hundred people to pay $20 a ticket for his thirty-first birthday party as a fundraiser for the charity. Then, he took the $15,000 they made and brought it immediately to a refugee camp in northern Uganda. They fixed three wells and sent the photos and the GPS coordinates back to the people who had given. The donors couldn't believe it; they had never heard of a charity following up on such a small donation. Some had forgotten they had even given.

The next year, he told people to stay home for his birthday and donate $32 instead. That year, he raised $59,000. Soon, others followed suit. A seven-year-old in Austin, Texas, raised $22,000. Justin Bieber raised $47,000. Twitter cofounder Jack Dorsey raised $174,000. Charity: water experimented—using any medium it could to get people to care and take action. With each experiment, it took

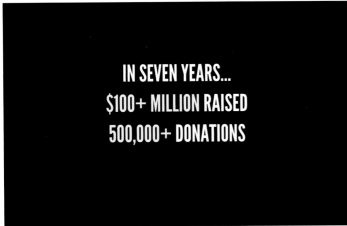

IN SEVEN YEARS...
$100+ MILLION RAISED
500,000+ DONATIONS

Images copyright Scott Harrison

what worked and found a way to expand it. By 2013, charity: water had brought clean water to 3.3 million people in twenty different countries. Yet, as impressive as that progress is, the need is still far greater. Scott has set a goal that by 2020, charity: water will have given 100 million people access to clean water. To get there, it is going to need help.

Charity: water's growth story contains four basic elements. Scott starts by describing the actions and experiments charity: water took to achieve its mission. Then, he tells how it followed up with those experiments by closing the loop with donors and taking what it learned and applying it to more experiments. Then, he shows how that learning has resulted in astounding results and progress. Finally, Scott shows how despite all that progress, charity: water still has a long way to go, and he invites people into the adventure to help achieve the vision.

Once you discovered your idea, what did you do about it? What happened after that? What needs to happen in the future? For founders, the venture story is the hub around which every other story turns. If the team members cannot translate their passion, understanding, and potential into a venture that produces measurable results, they are wasting their time.

The Elements of a Venture Growth Story

1. We took action.

2. We got results. We learned from those results and took more action.

3. This resulted in unbelievable progress.

4. For as much progress that's already been made, the vision for what we can do is bigger.

How to Tell a Great Story

A story has been the preferred medium of world changers since the beginning of history. Plato told stories. Jesus told stories. Abraham Lincoln told stories. Steve Jobs told stories. The difference between a great idea you've never heard of and one that's changed the world is its originator's ability to tell a damn good story. And, yet, stories are extremely simple.

This thing happened. Then, this other thing happened, which caused this other thing to happen, until finally something else happened as a result of all those things that had already happened. The end. So what makes stories so effective?

Stories aren't powerful because they are fancy; they are powerful because they are like life. They can't be boiled down to bullet points; they must be lived in and through time. With tools like MRI scans, we know now that by focusing on the details in a story—the world as we know it

through our five senses—a storyteller can literally create the event he or she describes inside the mind of the listener. When we describe the sweat dripping from an athlete's brow as he jogs beneath an August sun, parts of our brains light up as if we were actually out on the pavement with him.

As you incorporate stories into your pitch, you can increase their impact by paying attention to these characteristics of great stories.

What Makes a Great Story?

Things happen. For a story to be a story, things have to happen. Usually, one big thing happens and everything else in the story is in response to or a result of that one big thing. For the story of your pitch to be engaging, you'll have to choose the biggest and important events in your venture and describe those in a way in which each event builds on the other.

Your five senses give you access to vivid details. If you want to tell a story, you have to start where human knowledge begins: with the senses. As highly educated adults, we like to speak in abstractions, focusing on the ideas, concepts, and complex emotions that are the result of thousands of years of philosophy. We forget that no one has ever seen the wind blow. We see leaves turn, or feel a cool, intermittent pressure against our skin, or hear whistling all around us.

It's those sensory details that lead us to conclude that the wind is blowing.

To get your audience's attention, you must literally put them into the scene, letting them see what you see, feel what you feel, and hear what you hear. The more vivid the details in your story, the more likely they will stick in the mind of your audience.

Conflict. Life is about struggle, and stories should be, too. If there is no conflict in your story, the audience won't have anyone to root for. The point of a story is to get people to care. Nothing gets people to care like seeing someone they like face hardship.

Nancy Duarte's Sparkline

In her book *Resonate*, Nancy Duarte highlights another key characteristic about stories that is especially relevant for presentations: they contrast what is with what could be. The contour of a presentation as the speaker moves back and forth between what is and what could be is called a "sparkline," kind of like the heartbeat of the presentation. We use this technique throughout this book. Take the section on "Getting Clarity on Your Idea" in chapter 1:

Too often, people passionate about ideas have articulated them across scraps of paper, e-mails, and thoughts in their head. [what is] This constellation of notes looks a lot like the way the idea looks in your brain: thousands of neurons firing thoughts, making connections through synapses in a web of what were once disconnected memories and inputs. But if you want someone else to understand that mess of a web, you've got to find a way to get it into something more accessible. [what could be]

The sparkline happens at a more metalevel, too. The first half of the introduction was all about "what is" (fundraising is hard, experts give bad advice), but then the very first thing we do in chapter 1 is hit you with one big "what could be" (sharing everything that is world changing about your venture with others through a pitch deck). Great stories have a unique rhythm that carries the listener from the beginning and middle to the end, through a constant tension between what is and what could be.

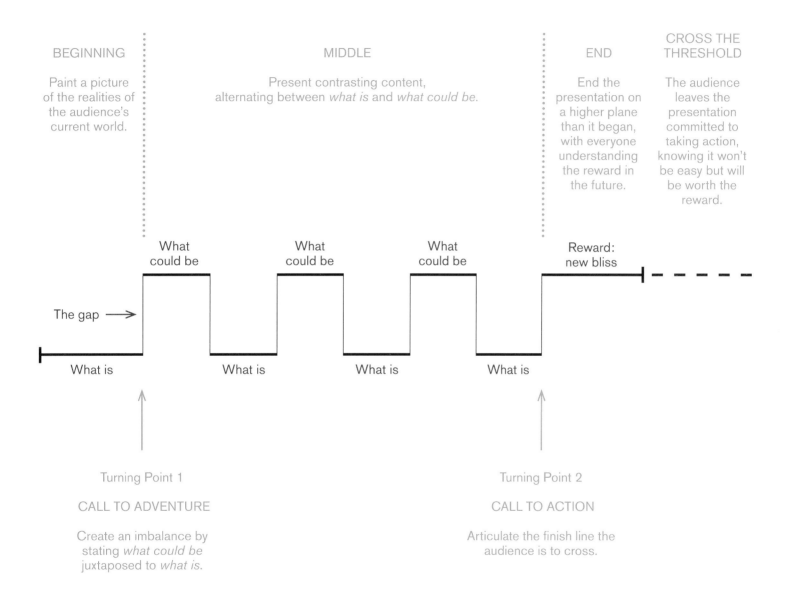

BEGINNING

Paint a picture of the realities of the audience's current world.

MIDDLE

Present contrasting content, alternating between *what is* and *what could be*.

END

End the presentation on a higher plane than it began, with everyone understanding the reward in the future.

CROSS THE THRESHOLD

The audience leaves the presentation committed to taking action, knowing it won't be easy but will be worth the reward.

What could be

What could be

What could be

Reward: new bliss

The gap →

What is

What is

What is

What is

Turning Point 1

CALL TO ADVENTURE

Create an imbalance by stating *what could be* juxtaposed to *what is*.

Turning Point 2

CALL TO ACTION

Articulate the finish line the audience is to cross.

Using Story to Craft the Arc of Your Pitch

You'll need to choose how to arrange the stories and the slides in your pitch. By leading with the stories and aspects of your venture that are the strongest, you can align your stories in a way that creates an interesting arc and captures the audience's attention.

Here are a few examples of how stories might fit into your pitch.

Origin Story	1. The Cover
	2. The Team
Industry Story	3. The Opportunity
Customer Story	4. The Problem
	5. The Solution
Venture Story	6. The Competition
	7. Your Advantage
	8. The Business Model
	9. The Financials
	10. The Ask

Origin story for:

- Products or services with high social benefit

- Effect: Taps into the audience's desire for meaning.

Customer story for:

- Complex products or services

- Customers with dramatic transformation stories

- Effect: Explains your venture and its value.

Industry story for:

- Disruptive products or services

- Effect: Shows you know what you're talking about and that the idea could be huge.

Venture story for:

- Ventures with immediate traction

- Effect: Feels like you're on a train that's headed somewhere big.

4

Design

The chapter on story was about the content of your pitch. Design is the tool you will use to help you tell that story.

The effectiveness of your pitch deck rests on its ability to communicate the brilliance of your venture clearly, compellingly, and immediately. Pitch decks are a visual medium; they use the power of visual thinking—a process of organizing, interpreting, and showing information spatially—to make an immense amount of information accessible and meaningful to an audience. Visual thinking engages the creative parts of our brain and allows us to see an idea or concept—even a very complex one—intuitively and simultaneously.

In this chapter, we will apply the best practices of visual thinking and design masters like Nancy Duarte, Dan Roam, and Scott McCloud to assemble a toolbox of design techniques and frameworks that help you bring your pitch deck to life.

Does This Stuff Really Matter?

A lot of entrepreneurs have asked us, "Do investors really care about what kind of fonts I use and the color of my slides?"

The short answer: Absolutely. Here's why.

1. **Investors are extremely busy.** They see hundreds, if not thousands, of pitches a year.

2. **The eye is faster than the mind.** Sight is our fastest sense, and subtle changes in color, shape, and style can dramatically affect our understanding of a subject and our opinion about it.

3. **Good design improves clarity.** People learn better when information is presented with great illustrations. Good design lets you communicate your story more easily and effectively.

4. **People are insulted when you give them trash.** Let them know you care enough to put time into what you ask them to read.

Key Elements:

- Layout

- Typography

- Color

- Images and photography

- Visualized data

Don't Do This

The state of enterprise mobile

- Mobile technology landscape is confusing and constantly changing
- Lines of business hiring mobile development shops to build apps outside of the IT department
- Enterprise IT not in control of the mobile architectural decisions
- Data and app security issues complicate the development of mobile apps
- Large enterprise systems having to spend years developing an API layer to fuel mobile initiatives
- More complex mobile apps must communicate with the enterprise system of record
- Customers, employees, and business are demanding more mobile apps
- Building mobile enterprise apps is too expensive and lengthy

---

- **No relationship between bullet points**

- **Inconsistent margins**

Do This

Fixing the world's broadband problem.

A network of networks. Our software bridges existing infrastructure to provide frictionless access to the Internet. We're moving your data from provider A to provider B. Our customers always interact with Karma.

- No bullet points

- Visualized data

- Consistent color scheme

There's something almost quite magical about visual information. It's effortless; it literally pours in. And if you're navigating a dense information jungle, coming across a beautiful graphic or a lovely data visualization, it's a relief, it's like coming across a clearing in the jungle.

—*David McCandless, data journalist and information designer*

Layout

How items are spaced in relation to each other and their background is one of the most important elements of good design. A grid allows you to arrange elements on your slide so that they look consistent and unified.

In her book *slide:ology*, Nancy Duarte discusses the idea of gridlines—crossing lines and rectangular boxes to give your slides a consistent structure. They work as an organizing principle to hang all of your content on. Here are some examples of different grid patterns used in decks throughout this book.

Place and lock the grid over each slide while you're arranging the elements in your pitch deck. When you finish, delete the grid from all but one extra slide at the back or front of your deck. You don't need to keep the same grid pattern every time, but you should know when you are breaking the pattern so that you can do it intentionally.

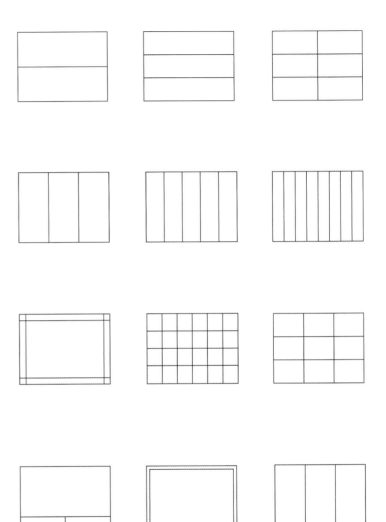

Typography

There's one thing you need to know about fonts: serifs. Serifs are those little feet that extend out of the edges of certain typefaces. In the words of one designer we spoke to, serifs are the "crown molding" of typeface. In the very old days when letters were chiseled into stone, the writers would use serifs to neaten and sharpen the ends of the lines they were creating, just as an architect would use molding to create a sharper edge in a room. In typefaces, when that little bit of crown molding is present, we call it a "serif" font. When it's absent, we call the font "sans serif" (that is, without serif).

Most designers will use two fonts for a project, one for titles and headings, and the other for body copy. Choosing one serif and one sans serif for those two fonts can create a nice sense of contrast. Our advice is to pick two to three favorites of each category and use those as your go-to fonts. Use one font for headlines and subheadings and another for blocks of text. There are few reasons to use any more than that. Fonts, like all good design, should be felt and not seen. Your fonts should reflect the personality you want to project. To make sure your font size is large enough, Duarte recommends that you measure the diagonal length of your screen, then stand back many feet and see if you can still read it. If you can, you've got the right font size.

Serif   Sans Serif

Color

The most basic building block of color is called hue. When we say that these colors are all "red" and these are all "blue," we are referring to the color's hue.

As you may remember from elementary school, there are six hues: red, orange, yellow, green, blue, violet.

But if there are only six, what makes for all the variety in color? Adding white (tint) or black (shade). We get all that wonderful and problematic variation in color from these two simple tools.

When it comes to your color palette, your focus should be on consistency or contrast. Colors that are too similar will make your design feel disorienting. And don't trust your eyes; get the RGB numbers. Create a slide at the beginning of your presentation that contains your color palette and stick with it.

The color palette for your deck should contain three core colors, a neutral color, and a highlight color. As you assemble your color palette, ask yourself: In the mind of my audience, which colors are associated with the thoughts, feelings, and ideas I want the audience to have? Of these colors, which relate well with my logo and with each other?

How to Hack Your Color Palette

Go to color.adobe.com, register on the site, click the camera icon, and upload an image of your current logo. If you don't have a logo yet, create a collage of a handful of photos that are representative of your industry and upload it as one image. The site will analyze your picture and create a color palette for you based on that image. Copy the RGB numbers of each color in the color palette and save them on a backup slide in your pitch deck. Presto! You have your color palette.

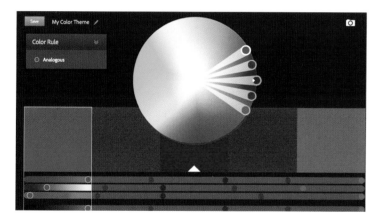

Images and Photography

Clear, defining images are one of the best ways to improve the design of your pitch deck. You can choose to use photos as a section of the slide or as the background, or simply show a photo on a slide with no words at all. Here are some keys to making the images in your deck sing.

Rule of Thirds

The rule of thirds is the magic trick of every good photographer, graphic designer, and artist. For some reason, our minds perceive greater energy and tension when the object of a photograph is focused around four key "crash points." You can visualize these crash points by dividing your photo into two sets of thirds, horizontally and vertically. The points at which those horizontal and vertical lines intersect are the crash points.

Types of Shots

Establishing shot. When introducing an environment or a place, photographers and filmmakers will use what's called an establishing shot. The goal in a shot like this is to orient the viewer to the scene by giving him a sense of the place as a whole. It may help to use an establishing shot in your pitch deck when you want to introduce an important place or environment that relates to your venture or as a way to begin to talk about your industry.

Medium shots. Think of medium shots as the distance at which you view things every day. With people, medium shots show most, and sometimes all, of the body. Medium shots are great for communicating an action that is occurring. If you want to show a process in action, a medium shot can be a great way to do it.

Close-ups. Close-ups show intensity. They highlight specific details of a photo or scene, such as an emotion or a feature or quality of a product. Close-ups can also convey intimacy and create direct experience.

Bleed. A photo that "bleeds" extends outside the frame into the space around it. You create bleeds by shooting or cropping images so that a portion of the image is cut out of the audience's view. You can use a bleed to break what visual artists call the fourth wall, the separation between the world of the piece and the world we are in.

The Use of the Center

Readers assign importance to characters and objects placed in the center. The center can also establish motion, communicate a mysterious balance, show the distance about to be crossed, show a distance already crossed, or imply an unseen object of a character's attention.

Stock Photography

If you're raising $1 million, your photos better look like $1 million. A good rule of thumb for using stock photography is that if the photograph would never happen in real life, don't use it. Bad photography distracts the viewer. If you have the budget, take the time to get a professional photograph or computer rendering of your product, your customers, and other unique aspects of your venture. If you don't, there are ways to get quality photos for cheap:

- **Free.** Use Google image search with the filter "Creative Commons" to find images you can post. Always include an attribution line for any photos you use that aren't your own. Simply add "© [Copyright Owner's Name]" to the bottom-right corner of your slide in small font. Sites like Unsplash and Death to the Stock Photo offer high-quality, free photography for use.

- **Cheap.** Stocksy and Creative Market sell quality stock photographs for as little as $10.

Resolution

Just like bad stock photography, photos with poor resolution hurt more than they help. For a full spread, look for images with a resolution of 1024 x 768.

Using Photos as Backgrounds

Increase the transparency on bold photos to help them fade into the background. You can also shade the area around the text to bring attention to your copy.

Visualized Data

Data visualization is a kind of visual storytelling; it takes viewers on a journey to show them why what they are seeing matters. In her book *slide:ology*, Duarte outlines a few keys to great data visualization. We've adapted them to create our top three.

Highlight What Matters

Emphasize the specific data and the conclusions you want someone to make from it. Change the color, zoom in, or use arrows.

Give Context

Look for ways to show how your numbers fit into a larger context. What percentage of the whole is that? How do your numbers compare to something the viewer is familiar with?

Stay Simple

Your data needs to be seen and understood in three seconds or less. If you think you might be trying to show too much at once, break it into more than one slide. Don't be afraid of simplicity and white space.

Data slides are not really about the data. They are about the meaning of the data.

—Nancy Duarte, author, slide:ology

Dan Roam's Five Ways of Showing

In his books *The Back of the Napkin* and *Blah Blah Blah*, Dan Roam divides every visual display of information into five basic types. Like the parts of a sentence, each of these visuals plays a different role in telling a story. Say goodbye to the bullet point. Here are your new ways of showing information. We use slides from Reaction, Inc.'s pitch deck to illustrate each way of showing.

1. Portraits

Visual representations of a person, place, or thing.

The nouns of visual thinking

Use to show: customer, solution

2. Maps

Show where things are.

The prepositions and conjunctions of visual thinking

Use to show: competition

3. Charts

Show how many things there are.

The adjectives of visual thinking

Use to show: market size, sales, and marketing

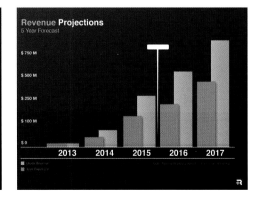

4. Timelines

Show when things happen.

The tense of visual thinking

Use to show: milestones

5. Flowcharts

Show how things happen. Combine a map and a timeline.

The complex verbs of visual thinking

Use to show: solution

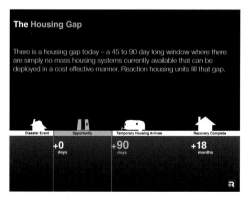

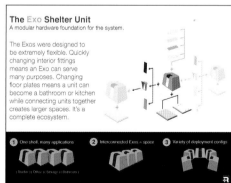

5

Text

This chapter is all about the words in your deck—what they should be, where they should be, and how they should change depending on your audience and environment. By paying attention to things like the voice and writing style of your text, you'll build a pitch deck that creates an experience that reflects your brand. The text in your deck must also do one more thing: communicate the data and evidence that will overcome doubt and push someone to action.

Key Elements:

- Writing style

- Voice and tone

- Format

- When words are not enough

Writing Style

Every communication medium carries a certain style with it. You write a love letter differently than you would write web copy or a legal contract. Pitch decks carry their own unique style, too, and that style has a lot to do with your audience, and where, when, and how they will see your deck.

Writing Style for Presentation Decks

A deck used as a visual aid during a presentation should have very few words—no more than one sentence per slide. Presentation decks also don't need to have complete sentences. Often, one word or a short phrase is enough to introduce the idea that you will carry forward. If you have already completed your reading deck, try deleting every word in it except for the headers and see if the words give enough context to still understand what the slide is about.

Writing Style for Reading Decks

With decks you plan to send to others to read, the slides have to do a lot of work to communicate everything you would have said in person. Your words have to catch their attention quickly, clearly communicate the basic point you want to put forth, back that point up with evidence, and then move on. Watch out for sentences that sound impressive but mean nothing. "We plan to pursue an effective marketing strategy" is a waste of time to read. If you create a slide for your marketing strategy, put the words "Marketing Strategy" in the corner and then write out your strategy in a sentence of fifteen words or less. If your strategy has multiple phases, create headings that describe each phase and then add short, straightforward explanations after those headings. Reading decks should also be "scanning" decks. If I only have fifteen seconds to look through the whole thing, I should still be able to get a pretty good idea of what it is about.

George Orwell's Rules for Writing

George Orwell, the famous author of *Animal Farm* and *1984*, wrote a list of rules for writing in his 1946 essay, "Politics and the English Language." Treat these six rules as your bible; they will make you a significantly better writer overnight.

1. Never use a metaphor, simile, or other figure of speech which you are used to seeing in print.

2. Never use a long word where a short one will do.

3. If it is possible to cut a word out, always cut it out.

4. Never use the passive ["was saved"] where you can use the active ["saved"].

5. Never use a foreign phrase, a scientific word, or a jargon word if you can think of an everyday English equivalent.

6. Break any of these rules sooner than say anything outright barbarous.

Voice and Tone

Voice and tone show the personality of your deck. If Amazon wanted to publish your pitch deck as an audio book, who would it get to read it? James Earl Jones? Tina Fey? Justin Timberlake? How do you want people to feel when they are reading your deck? Should they be smiling? Should their brows be furrowed with passion or intense concentration? You have the power to decide what experience your audience has with the kind of voice and tone you use.

Word Choice

To establish your voice and tone, start with the words you choose. Are they formal or informal? Do you use a lot of words that end with the "shun" sound (execution, completion, formation)? Do you want to use slang?

Sentence Structure

Take a look at the punctuation we use in this book. We have a lot of shorter, simple sentences that only communicate one idea at a time. Sometimes, we add in asides using em dashes—like we're doing now—or commas that make the sentence sound more conversational.

Metaphors and Imagery

What do people see in their heads when they read your words? Should you use military metaphors (like "capture the first beachhead") or organic metaphors (like "plant and grow new markets")?

Format

When you first saw the previous page, one of the things you likely noticed right way was "Voice and Tone" in big letters. You knew that this section was going to have something to do with voice and tone because the way the copy was arranged told you that. You also knew that a concept like word choice was related to voice and tone, probably as one aspect of voice and tone. You knew that because the phrase "Word Choice" was placed in bold, on its own line, in a font size that is bigger than the rest of the text but smaller than the heading "Voice and Tone." You can make all of these conclusions because of the formatting of the text on the page.

Formatting is the appearance of the design or layout of the actual words on the page and within a paragraph or sentence. Your formatting will change slightly for your presentation deck and your reading deck.

Common Formatting for Reading Decks

- Capture the audience's attention in the top third of the slide. Use titles or short phrases to give just enough information for someone to understand what the slide is about in less than three seconds.

- Reading decks often contain three content elements: a title, a short phrase or sentence laying out the core argument of the slide, and a larger 1–3 sentence paragraph with further explanation or evidence.

- Word economy still matters. Use as few words as possible.

- Think graphic novel.

Common Formatting for Presentation Decks

- The fewer the words, the better. Limit each slide to ten words max. Who says you need any text at all?

- If you are not sure about whether to include something, imagine you are a grandparent and are trying to read the slides from the very back of the room.

- If you already created your reading deck, start your presentation deck by deleting every word except the title.

- Think Steve Jobs.

When Words Are Not Enough

One of Walt Disney's dreams was to have rides where live animals interacted in close proximity with the guests. Imagine the experience of a real safari—elephants and giraffes so close to you that you could see the individual strands of their fur. But there were too many technical and safety obstacles, so he had to settle for those goofy animatronic animals. Fast forward a half-century. Michael Eisner, now CEO of Disney, was participating in the last round of discussions for a soon-to-be-built new theme park: Magic Kingdom. Finally, Walt's dream might be realized. But Eisner couldn't see what the big deal was. What's so special about a live animal?

Joe Rhode, the lead Imagineer on the project, gave the final pitch to the Disney executives. "We know that there are concerns about whether animals are, in and of themselves, dramatic," he began.

"The heart of the Animal Kingdom park is animals, and our guests' encounters with them. We have gone to great lengths to make sure that the animals will be displayed in a way that will bring them and people together as never before . . . ," he continued.

Then a door opened and in walked a 400-pound Bengal tiger. While Rhode continued his presentation as if nothing had happened, the tiger walked around the table, sniffing the bewildered executives.

End of discussion.

Your evidence will not speak for itself. You must find ways to make that evidence compelling and real to your audience.

For example, Freight Farms, an agricultural startup that turns used shipping containers into automated hydroponic farms, would always bring investors into a freight farm before it asked them to invest. Paradigm, a social business that sells highly efficient stoves to women in the developing world, would tie a huge bundle of sticks together—the same size that a women in a developing country would carry for miles to use for fuel—and would challenge investors to try to carry it on their backs. Many couldn't.

What will create a visceral experience in the minds of your audience? What will make them feel the power of what you are doing and motivate them to do something about it? Turn the page, and imagine, as an investor, seeing that walk into the room.

Enough said.

How to Start
Your Deck

1. Draw ten rectangles and put the name of each slide at the top.

Divide a whiteboard or a piece of paper into ten rectangles and treat each rectangle as a slide. Put the titles of each slide at the top. Then, sketch out the storyline of your pitch in words and pictures. The image to the right is a photo of one of our original outlines of the pitch deck for this book.

2. Tweet the big ideas

Turn the ten building blocks into a Twitter-size phrase that describes that aspect of your venture. You can also use visuals to describe each aspect.

3. Ask yourself: If I were to insert my most compelling story about my venture, what story would I tell?

Use that story to craft the arc of your deck and the order of your slides. You can open with that story to hook your audience, or you can build toward it as the climax.

How to Send Your Deck

The type of file you send as an attachment or the kind of paper you print your deck on may seem like a minor detail. It's not. The way you send your deck dictates what kind of first impression your deck will make on others. You have invested a lot of work to get your deck ready to send to others; you don't want all of that work wasted because they can't open the file or are distracted by the terrible stapling.

Tips for a Printed Deck

Proper binding. Steel binding is the best and most expensive, but it can be hard to find a print shop with the machine to do it. If that is unavailable, then we recommend spiral binding. Comb binding is okay, but has a tendency to fall apart. If this sounds confusing, your local print shop will be able to set you in the right direction. Never use a staple!

Good paper. Use twenty-eight- or thirty-two-pound paper. The twenty-two- and twenty-four-pound paper feels cheap and gives you hellish paper cuts.

A full deck and a one-pager. The one-pager should contain each element of your deck but on one page for easy viewing.

Tips for a Digital Deck

PDF, *not* Keynote. Always convert your deck into PDF format rather than a Word, Keynote, or PowerPoint document. Editable documents are messy, don't always open, and are much too large.

Controlled access. There's little you can do to prevent people from sharing your deck if they really want to. Password-protecting the PDF can keep your deck from ending up in the wrong hands. You can also use docsend.com (Google Analytics for documents), which will tell you who read your deck and how long it took them.

Updates and versions. Instead of attaching your deck to an e-mail, consider hosting it on Dropbox and sending only the link in your e-mails. This way you can keep your deck updated and the investor will always see the latest version. When you save a new version, keep an archive of the old one in a separate folder so you can keep track of the changes you've made.

6

Actual Pitch Decks

You're about to see what only venture capitalists and investors typically get to see: excerpts from the actual pitch decks and fundraising strategies of fifteen successfully funded startups. For this chapter, we profile ventures from across multiple sectors, stages, and cities. Combined, these ventures have raised well over $100 million.

We debated whether to include this chapter at all; people find it nerve-racking to show their investor decks. But in the spirit of giving back, the founders featured here have chosen to offer you something that they normally never show anyone. We are deeply grateful for their commitment to advancing entrepreneurship.

As these profiles illustrate, when it comes to fundraising, there is no one-size-fits-all template, but there are patterns and principles to identify. Aside from the founders' own comments and advice, we let their decks speak for themselves.

Drum roll please . . . Here are the strategies and materials of fifteen ventures that crushed it at raising money.

Able Lending · Low-interest loans to small businesses.

Founding team: Evan Baehr, Will Davis
Location: Austin, TX
Funding round: Series A
Market category: finance; banking

Able is a set of engineers, math geeks, designers, and business consultants that together built a new way to fund "the Fortune 5 million"—the 5 million small businesses in the United States that create two-thirds of all jobs, but can't access reasonably priced capital. The deck is clean with simple, to-the-point visuals. It's also text-heavy, with the bottom third of the slide often used to explain the specifics of the Able model. This structure, combined with large and phrase-length titles, lets the reader understand each slide quickly, but then dig in if and when they want more.

Common Mistakes Founders Make
"Their decks are usually terrible. They wait to meet investors until they need money. They are too tense and fail to build positive rapport with investors."

Advice
"Build a deck early and then use it to refine your business model over time."

Redo
"I'd find a way to answer some of the most common objections early on. Also, we often ended up scrapping the deck in our pitches and instead writing four core graphs on the board. The deck should start with those."

Slide Investors Focused on Most
"The amortization slide, though a bit technical, is actually the core of the model."

MEETINGS

Number of investor meetings

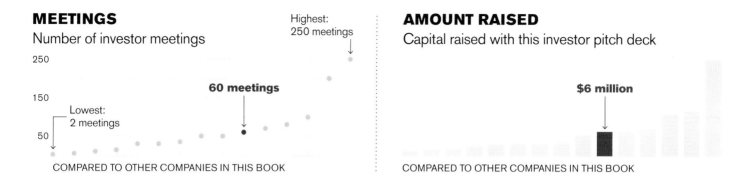

Highest:
250 meetings

250

60 meetings

150

Lowest:
2 meetings

50

COMPARED TO OTHER COMPANIES IN THIS BOOK

AMOUNT RAISED

Capital raised with this investor pitch deck

$6 million

COMPARED TO OTHER COMPANIES IN THIS BOOK

TIMING

1 year, 8 months

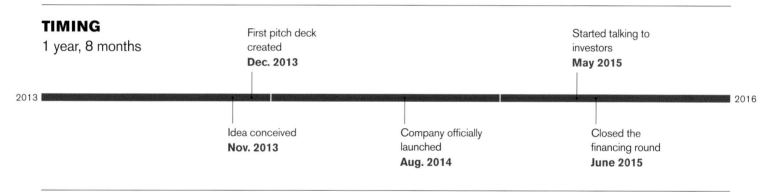

First pitch deck
created
Dec. 2013

Started talking to
investors
May 2015

2013

2016

Idea conceived
Nov. 2013

Company officially
launched
Aug. 2014

Closed the
financing round
June 2015

INVESTORS

Number of investors

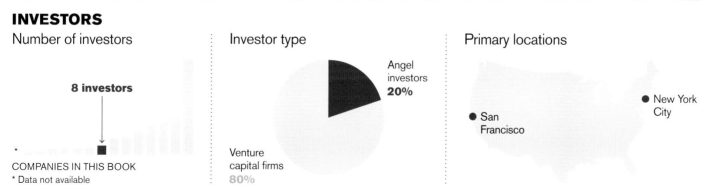

8 investors

*

COMPANIES IN THIS BOOK
* Data not available

Investor type

Angel
investors
20%

Venture
capital firms
80%

Primary locations

● New York
City

● San
Francisco

Cover

Problem (Small Businesses)

Small business want credit, can't get it

5,700,000: number of small businesses in the United States (SMBs):
- create **65%** of all jobs in US
- **employ 50%** of workforce

75% of "fortune five million" is not even applying for (or has applied and cannot get) the credit they desire

Banks have abandoned SMBs:
- bank consolidation eroded community banks (14,000 down to 7,000 in last 20 years), acquisition costs very high
- regulatory overhang powerful

Result?
- **SMBs are dying—this year we'll lose 75,000 SMBs.** In only 6 of last 40 years have more SMBs been destroyed than created—each year since 2008.
- Going concern **SMBs are not growing**: 42% wanted to expand but couldn't, 18% couldn't hire, 16% couldn't complete existing orders
- in this environment, **big, old companies win**

Problem (Lenders)

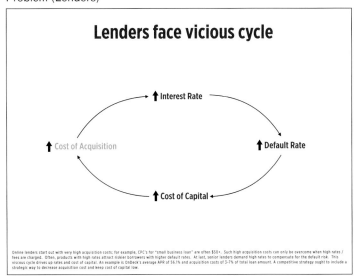

Lenders face vicious cycle

↑ Interest Rate

↑ Cost of Acquisition

↑ Default Rate

↑ Cost of Capital

Online lenders start out with very high acquisition costs; for example, CPC's for "small business loan" are often $50+. Such high acquisition costs can only be overcome when high rates / fees are charged. Often, products with high rates attract riskier borrowers with higher default rates. At last, senior lenders demand high rates to compensate for the default risk. This viscous cycle drives up rates and cost of capital. An example is OnDeck's average APR of 56.1% and acquisition costs of 3-7% of total loan amount. A competitive strategy ought to include a strategic way to decrease acquisition cost and keep cost of capital low.

Competition

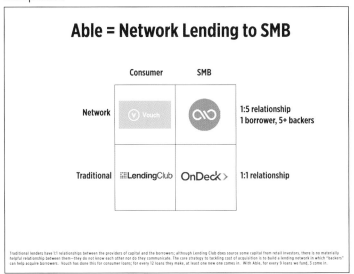

Able = Network Lending to SMB

	Consumer	SMB	
Network	Vouch	able	1:5 relationship 1 borrower, 5+ backers
Traditional	LendingClub	OnDeck	1:1 relationship

Traditional lenders have 1:1 relationships between the providers of capital and the borrowers; although Lending Club does source some capital from retail investors, there is no materially helpful relationship between them—they do not know each other nor do they communicate. The core strategy to tackling cost of acquisition is to build a lending network in which "backers" can help acquire borrowers. Vouch has done this for consumer loans; for every 12 loans they make, at least one new one comes in. With Able, for every 9 loans we fund, 3 come in.

Unique Value Proposition

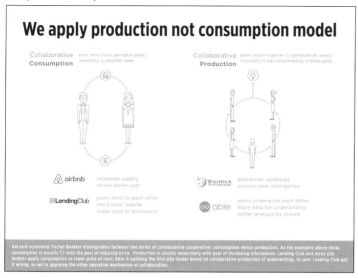

Solution

Case Study

How It Works

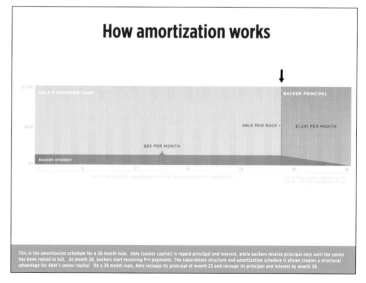

Beacon • All-you-can-fly subscription air service.

Founding team: Wade Eyerly, Cory Cozzens, Reed Farnsworth, Ryan Morley
Location: New York City
Funding round: Series A
Market category: travel

Three of the four founders of Beacon had already built one company that was the first to apply the subscription model to aviation—Surf Air—and led the first three rounds for the company that has now raised $88 million. In their deck, the team struck an excellent balance in communicating the right kind of information simply and effectively.

Common Mistakes Founders Make

"They think that success raising money defines them as entrepreneurs. It doesn't. Build your business. This bleeds into the process, as they hyperfocus on new metrics that they can share. The problem is that no amount of data will compel an investor to invest. What you have to do is tell a narrative. You have to sell the story that you're onto something big and that you're the team that can do it."

Advice

"Know what you're good at and do it. Know what you're not and be honest about it. Don't gloss over failures, holes on your team, things that didn't work out, etc. Investors don't care that you took a swing at something and it didn't work out. They also aren't worried that your team has holes in it. They do care that you know it, however. If you're so focused on having all the answers, you'll come across as unaware of the challenges ahead of you."

Redo

"I would spend less time building it. Making the deck is a good exercise for founders and helps focus your narrative and your thinking, but no one invests in a deck."

Slide Investors Focused on Most

"I'm not sure investors even look at it. I use the deck as an e-mail attachment prior to meeting with them and never actually open it when we're together. I know the information inside out, so we just have a conversation. I can answer the questions they actually have, as opposed to driving the conversation to answer the questions that I anticipated them having when we built the deck."

MEETINGS

Number of investor meetings

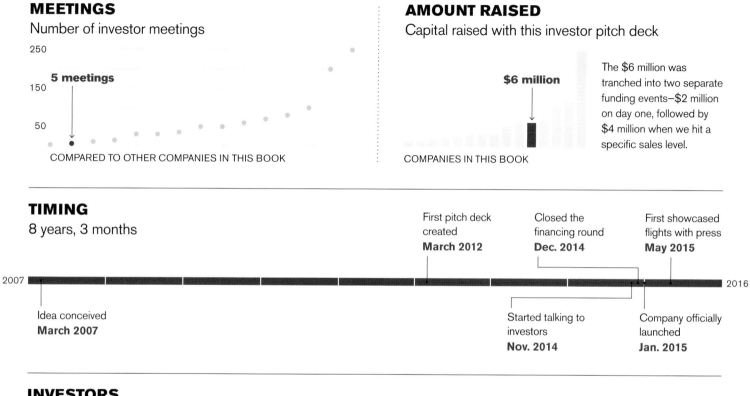

250

5 meetings

150

50

COMPARED TO OTHER COMPANIES IN THIS BOOK

AMOUNT RAISED

Capital raised with this investor pitch deck

$6 million

The $6 million was tranched into two separate funding events—$2 million on day one, followed by $4 million when we hit a specific sales level.

COMPANIES IN THIS BOOK

TIMING

8 years, 3 months

First pitch deck created
March 2012

Closed the financing round
Dec. 2014

First showcased flights with press
May 2015

2007

Idea conceived
March 2007

Started talking to investors
Nov. 2014

Company officially launched
Jan. 2015

2016

INVESTORS

Number of investors

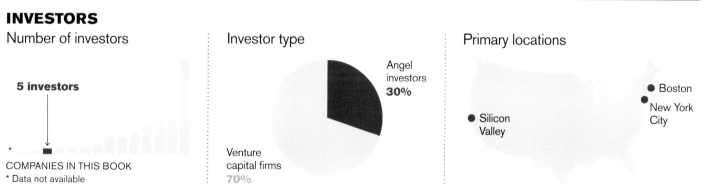

5 investors

*
COMPANIES IN THIS BOOK
* Data not available

Investor type

Angel investors
30%

Venture capital firms
70%

Primary locations

Boston

New York City

Silicon Valley

Cover

Product

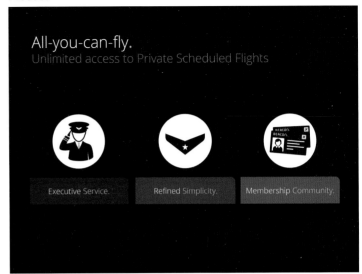

All-you-can-fly.
Unlimited access to Private Scheduled Flights

Executive Service.　　Refined Simplicity.　　Membership Community.

Team

Our Team/History.

WADE
FOUNDER
& FMR CEO,
SURF AIR

REED
FOUNDER
& FMR CFO,
SURF AIR

CORY
FOUNDER
& FMR SVP,
SURF AIR

RYAN
FMR DEPUTY
FINANCE DIRECTOR
MITT ROMNEY FOR
PRESIDENT

We know subscription airlines and sales

Financials

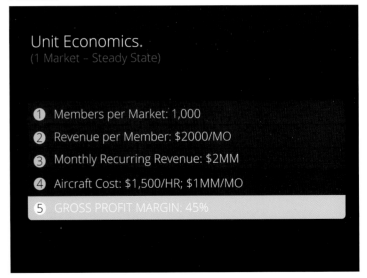

Unit Economics.
(1 Market – Steady State)

1. Members per Market: 1,000
2. Revenue per Member: $2000/MO
3. Monthly Recurring Revenue: $2MM
4. Aircraft Cost: $1,500/HR; $1MM/MO
5. GROSS PROFIT MARGIN: 45%

Timeline

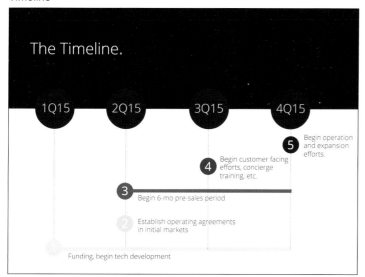

Customer Acquisition Strategy

Growth Plan

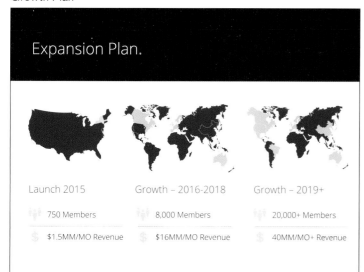

The Ask

Connect · Global messaging platform.

Founding team: Ryan Allis, Caen Contee, Anima Sarah LaVoy, Zachary Melamed
Location: San Francisco, CA
Funding round: Series A
Market category: mobile; messaging

Connect is cofounder Ryan Allis's second venture. He helped grow his first startup, iContact, to 300 employees and $50 million in annual sales and sold it in 2012. Ryan's commitment to relationships has led him to become one of the most well-connected entrepreneurs around. Connect focused on building a business with significant traction before they raised money, which is reflected in their deck.

Common Mistakes Founders Make

"Raising too much money, too early on. I often see companies raising tens of millions of dollars now, before they've proven the value proposition, which makes their monthly net losses too high and forces them to continue to raise more and more money. Also, entrepreneurs don't take the time to understand the environment in which they're operating. If you don't understand your industry's history and can't tie that together with what you're building today, then investors will think that you haven't done your research."

Advice

"Keep your costs low and raise very little money, under $50,000, until you know that you have something. Unless you have $10,000 a month in recurring revenue or 10,000 daily active users, don't raise outside capital. Take consulting gigs or freelance work on the side; work as a barista; keep your day job; whatever you have to do to keep your costs super-low until you have product-market fit and active engaged users. Once you have that, then you ramp up."

Redo

"I would have waited even longer to raise our first outside round of capital. We had 1.5 million users when we raised our Series A. However, we still had a few more risks to get past in order to achieve true product-market fit. In hindsight, I would have waited to invest in marketing and advertising until we had retention really nailed."

Slide Investors Focused on Most

"'Monthly Active User Trends' and 'Total Usage Trends.'"

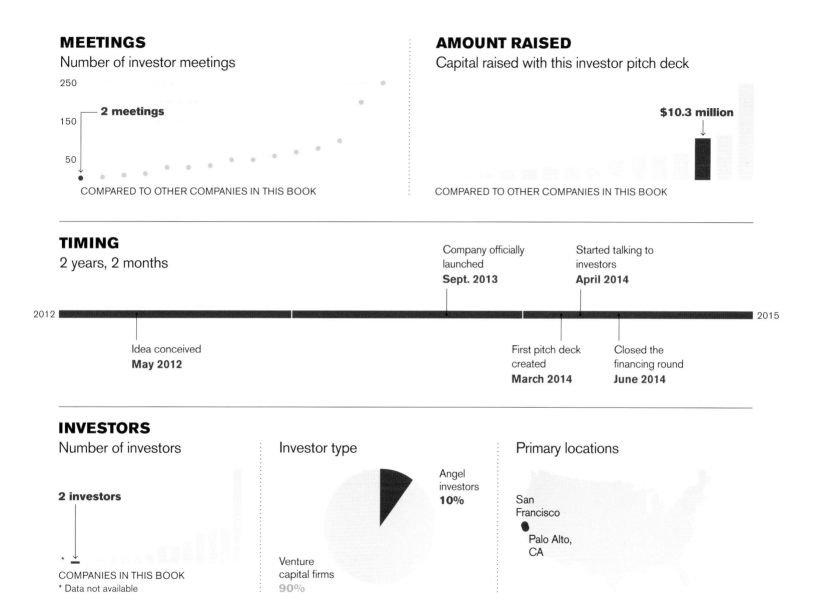

MEETINGS
Number of investor meetings

250

2 meetings

150

50

COMPARED TO OTHER COMPANIES IN THIS BOOK

AMOUNT RAISED
Capital raised with this investor pitch deck

$10.3 million

COMPARED TO OTHER COMPANIES IN THIS BOOK

TIMING
2 years, 2 months

Company officially
launched
Sept. 2013

Started talking to
investors
April 2014

2012 ————————————————————————————————— 2015

Idea conceived
May 2012

First pitch deck
created
March 2014

Closed the
financing round
June 2014

INVESTORS
Number of investors

2 investors

*
COMPANIES IN THIS BOOK
* Data not available

Investor type

Angel
investors
10%

Venture
capital firms
90%

Primary locations

San
Francisco

Palo Alto,
CA

Cover

Traction

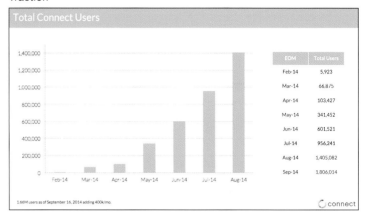

Unique Value Proposition

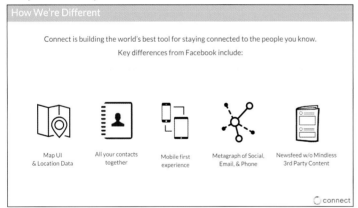

Solution

Competition

Team

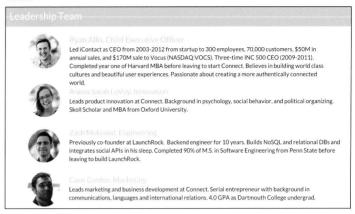

Milestones

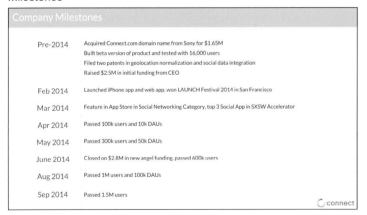

Press

Contactually · Contactually helps professionals turn relationships into results.

Founding team: Zvi Band, Jeff Carbonella, Tony Cappaert
Location: Washington, DC
Funding round: Series seed
Market category: sales and marketing, customer relationship management

Contactually is a customer relationship management software that aggregates online communication and interaction in order to help users maintain relationships with important contacts. Cofounded by Zvi Band and Tony Cappaert, Contactually got an early boost in 2011 when it was backed by the accelerator 500 Startups. The team then used that momentum to raise $3 million over two rounds of funding. The deck relies on a combination of short, digestible copy and graphics.

Common Mistakes Founders Make
"Don't pitch everyone. Focus just on the investors for whom your company is in their wheelhouse. Also, don't be afraid to ask for a clear path forward and a yes or no."

Advice
"Enjoy it. Every part of the company, including fundraising, should be a fun and exciting experience. If you are hating it or feel your back is up against the wall, change things."

Redo
"I would focus a lot more on the narrative. We spent a lot of time talking about data and checking the boxes of what's in a VC pitch. But we spent very little time thinking about crafting a concise narrative for what we've built and where we're going."

Slide Investors Focused on Most
"Product, market, competition."

MEETINGS

Number of investor meetings

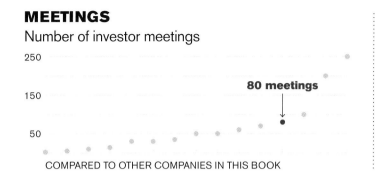

80 meetings

250

150

50

COMPARED TO OTHER COMPANIES IN THIS BOOK

AMOUNT RAISED

Capital raised with this investor pitch deck

$3 million
(over two rounds)

COMPARED TO OTHER COMPANIES IN THIS BOOK

TIMING

1 year, 1 month

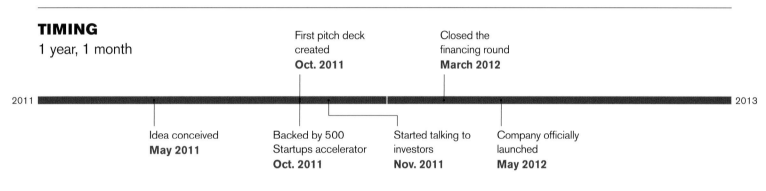

First pitch deck
created
Oct. 2011

Closed the
financing round
March 2012

2011

2013

Idea conceived
May 2011

Backed by 500
Startups accelerator
Oct. 2011

Started talking to
investors
Nov. 2011

Company officially
launched
May 2012

INVESTORS

Number of investors

6 investors

*

COMPANIES IN THIS BOOK
* Data not available

Investor type

Accelerators
5%

Angel
investors
10%

Venture
capital firms
85%

Primary locations

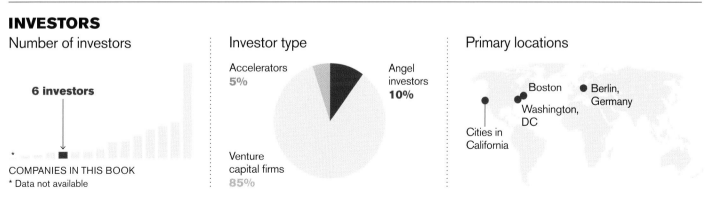

Boston

Berlin,
Germany

Washington,
DC

Cities in
California

Cover

Overview

Investment Highlights

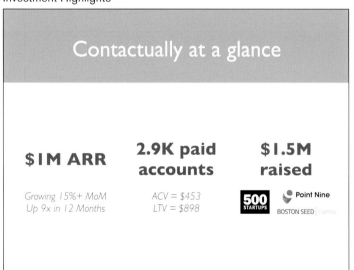

How It Works

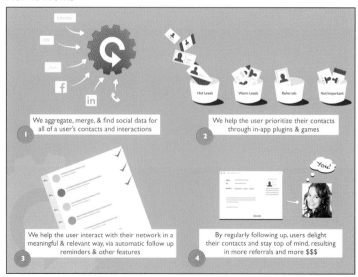

Traction

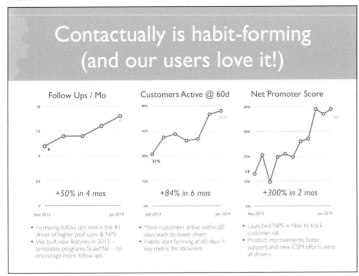

Customer Acquisition Strategy

Competition

The Ask

We're raising a $5M Series A with three goals

1. **Ramp up sales**: Scale inside sales team and develop outbound sales practice

2. **Optimize the platform for scale & ROI**: Improve performance & deliver value, esp for teams

3. **Emphasize thought leadership**: Drive lead gen via content marketing and partnerships

DocSend • DocSend tells you what happens to your documents after you send them.

Founding team: Russ Heddleston, Dave Koslow, Tony Cassanego
Location: San Francisco, CA
Funding round: Series seed
Market category: software

Armed with computer science degrees from Stanford and experience working at companies like Facebook and Dropbox, Russ Heddleston, Tony Cassanego, and Dave Koslow founded DocSend, a service that tracks everything that happens to a document after you share it. The service became a hit among people sharing pitch decks themselves. DocSend's deck is heavy on copy and uses neutral colors to avoid drawing attention away from the words.

Common Mistakes Founders Make

"It's all about quality, not quantity. Create a list of thirty investors who you actually want to meet with. Set up at least twenty meetings in a two-week period. Do this at least a few weeks out. If you can't get any of those twenty to invest, you need to change something before you try again."

Advice

"Focus on your strengths. Be sure to tell investors why you're different and be sure to bring something unique to the table. This could be a hundred interviews with potential customers, it could be 10,000 signups, or it could be your background of ten years building machine learning software."

Redo

"The design on this deck is atrocious. Our newer deck looks a ton better. We also have a lot more detail on our target user."

Slide Investors Focused on Most

"The team slide was viewed the longest on average, followed by the competition slide."

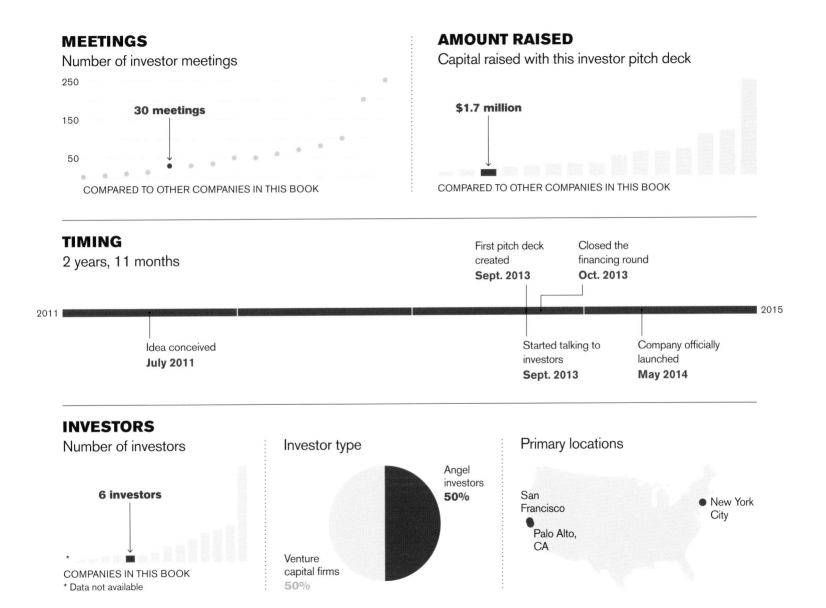

MEETINGS

Number of investor meetings

250

30 meetings

150

50

COMPARED TO OTHER COMPANIES IN THIS BOOK

AMOUNT RAISED

Capital raised with this investor pitch deck

$1.7 million

COMPARED TO OTHER COMPANIES IN THIS BOOK

TIMING

2 years, 11 months

First pitch deck created
Sept. 2013

Closed the financing round
Oct. 2013

2011

Idea conceived
July 2011

Started talking to investors
Sept. 2013

Company officially launched
May 2014

2015

INVESTORS

Number of investors

6 investors

*

COMPANIES IN THIS BOOK
* Data not available

Investor type

Angel investors
50%

Venture capital firms
50%

Primary locations

San Francisco

Palo Alto, CA

New York City

Cover

Team

Overview

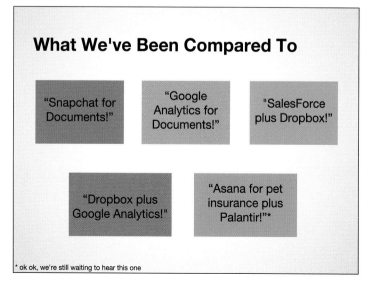

How It Works

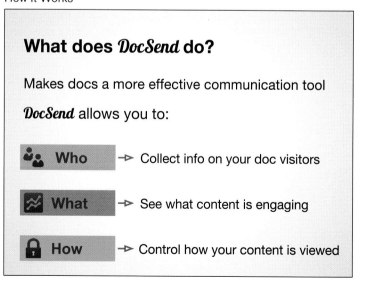

Problem

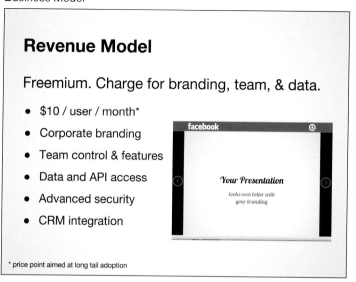

Today's issues with external doc sharing

Who in an organization is viewing

- Did the CEO get to see my presentation?
- Who in the organization looked at the follow up material I sent?

What are visitors engaging with

- Which pages do visitors spend the most time viewing?
- Is my document too long? Are later pages viewed less?

How to control the visitor experience

- Leverage your company's branding in the doc viewer.
- Know when it's the right time to engage the client.

Business Model

Revenue Model

Freemium. Charge for branding, team, & data.

- $10 / user / month*
- Corporate branding
- Team control & features
- Data and API access
- Advanced security
- CRM integration

facebook

Your Presentation

looks even better with your branding

* price point aimed at long tail adoption

Competition

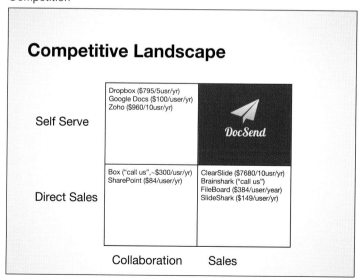

Competitive Landscape

	Collaboration	Sales
Self Serve	Dropbox ($795/5usr/yr) Google Docs ($100/user/yr) Zoho ($960/10usr/yr)	*DocSend*
Direct Sales	Box ("call us",~$300/usr/yr) SharePoint ($84/user/yr)	ClearSlide ($7680/10usr/yr) Brainshark ("call us") FileBoard ($384/user/year) SlideShark ($149/user/yr)

Screenshot

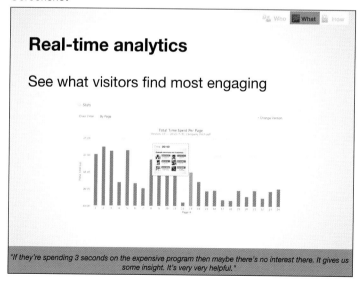

Who   What   How

Real-time analytics

See what visitors find most engaging

"If they're spending 3 seconds on the expensive program then maybe there's no interest there. It gives us some insight. It's very very helpful."

First Opinion · A qualified doctor available 24/7 at no cost.

Founding team: McKay Thomas, Jay Marcyes
Location: San Francisco, CA
Funding round: Series seed
Market category: parenting; health and wellness; mobile health

First Opinion lets parents, specifically young moms, track their children's health issues and gives them the ability to connect them with a doctor when necessary. Founder McKay Thomas included pictures of him and his children in the deck, making the story more personal and compelling.

Common Mistakes Founders Make

"Build relationships; don't pitch your business. I have fond memories with nearly every person who invested in my seed, and that's no coincidence. Keep your deck in your bag; rather, make a new friend with the person across from you. You've got thirty minutes to make yourself memorable, and it's not in your deck. It's you. You are what makes your business special at the seed stage. Make sure whomever you're meeting with feels that."

Advice

"Be the most genuine, thoughtful, loving version of yourself. And speak with so much passion that you'll be the only person on their mind for the next ten years. There's a lot of talk in this book about decks, but my lasting advice is to keep your hands on the table, not on your iPad. Keep your eyes locked on the person you're meeting with, not on a slide. Talk about them and their family and what they find interesting, not your business. Make them bring up your business. Be honest. Be yourself. Set out to make a friendship, not a business deal, and you'll likely find both."

Redo

"I'd add more substantiated data about the target market (new parents) and the total addressable market (urgent care, primary care). I'd also shorten the explanation of the product and make it even more emotional."

Slide Investors Focused on Most

" 'The Market in the Middle' slide explains what I intend to accomplish with First Opinion and at the same time explains why no one has created this product before. When you look at the market size on either end, it's clear there's a ton of value to be captured."

MEETINGS
Number of investor meetings

250

35 meetings

150

50

COMPARED TO OTHER COMPANIES IN THIS BOOK

AMOUNT RAISED
Capital raised with this investor pitch deck

$2.6 million

COMPARED TO OTHER COMPANIES IN THIS BOOK

TIMING
2 years, 3 months

First pitch deck
created
Dec. 2012

Located
cofounder
June 2013

Closed the
financing round
Dec. 2013

Brought on chief
operating officer
March 2014

2012

2015

Idea conceived
Jan. 2012

Started talking to
investors
Dec. 2012

Company officially
launched
Dec. 2013

INVESTORS
Number of investors

14 investors

*

COMPANIES IN THIS BOOK
* Data not available

Investor type

Friends and
family
0.5%

Angel
investors
4%

Venture
capital firms
95.5%

Primary locations

Chicago

San
Francisco

São Paulo,
Brazil

Cover

Team

Problem

Solution

Opportunity

Customer

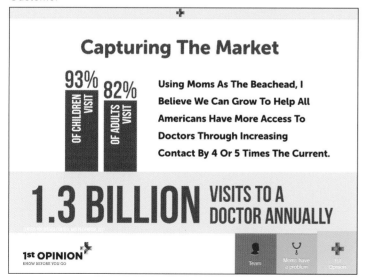

Customer Acquisition Strategy

The Ask

Freight Farms · **Everything to allow anyone, anywhere, to become a producer of local, sustainable greens and herbs.**

Founding team: Brad McNamara, Jonathan Friedman
Location: Boston, MA
Funding round: Series A
Market category: Internet of Things; mobile commerce; agriculture

You might not think of Boston as farmland, but Freight Farms cofounders Brad McNamara and Jonathan Friedman created a product that enables anyone to grow farm-fresh produce year-round. By building and selling their product before trying to raise capital, they were able to prove there's a market for what they were making. Clean, crisp pictures combined with straightforward, short copy help grab and keep a reader's attention and let the product speak for itself.

Common Mistakes Founders Make
"All the same mistakes we made. Listening to the press, reading your own clippings (or lack thereof), not listening to the right people, listening to the wrong people. Biggest mistake (we avoided this one) is losing sight of what you ultimately are *going* to accomplish. To convince people to invest, you'll need to do a lot of nitty-gritty detail stuff, business modeling, etc., that can derail your original plan. Try to check back in with your cofounder often enough and call each other on the BS. To that end, the best advice is to have a great cofounding team."

Advice
"Build and sell it first, then look for money. If you can sell your dream and prototype for real money, it's much easier."

Redo
"I wouldn't change anything; all the information and style were reflective of where we were as a company at that stage."

Slide Investors Focused on Most
"The slides that provoked the most discussion were the sales, business model, and customer economic returns slides."

MEETINGS

Number of investor meetings

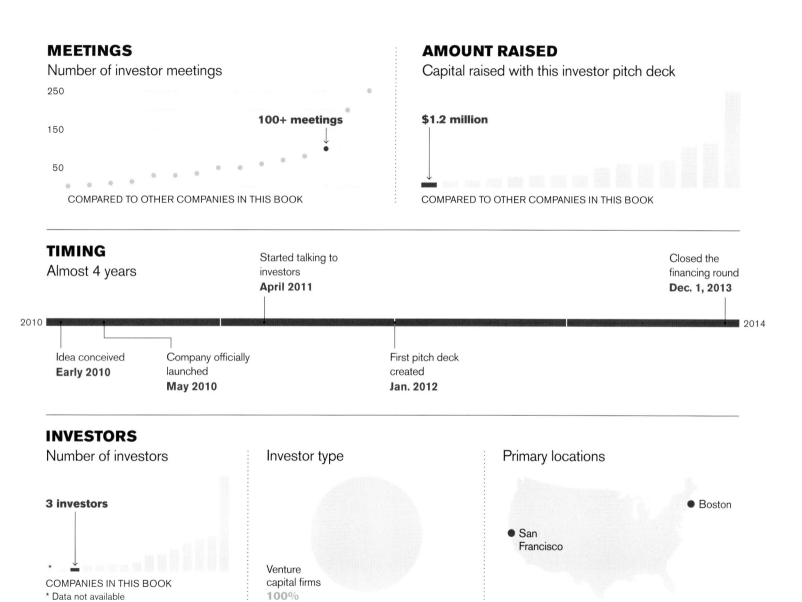

250

150

50

100+ meetings

COMPARED TO OTHER COMPANIES IN THIS BOOK

AMOUNT RAISED

Capital raised with this investor pitch deck

$1.2 million

COMPARED TO OTHER COMPANIES IN THIS BOOK

TIMING

Almost 4 years

Started talking to
investors
April 2011

Closed the
financing round
Dec. 1, 2013

2010

2014

Idea conceived
Early 2010

Company officially
launched
May 2010

First pitch deck
created
Jan. 2012

INVESTORS

Number of investors

3 investors

*

COMPANIES IN THIS BOOK
* Data not available

Investor type

Venture
capital firms
100%

Primary locations

● Boston

● San
Francisco

Cover

Opportunity

Mission

Unique Value Proposition

Product

THE **LGM**

(LEAFY GREEN MACHINE)

- Ready to grow 1200 heads per week
- Fresh produce 365 days a year
- 95% Less Water Use vs. Conventional
- Delivered Fully Assembled
- Easy to Use + Fast Learning Curve
- Automated Climate Mgmt
- 1800ft of Production inside 320sqft

Product

farmhand

- Connect to your farm from anywhere
- 24/7 access and visibility to your farm
- Monitor Water and Climate conditions
- Receive Alerts and Notifications
- View live in-farm video
- Grow your market with the farmhand hotspot
- Data logging
- Food Safety Mgmt

Customer

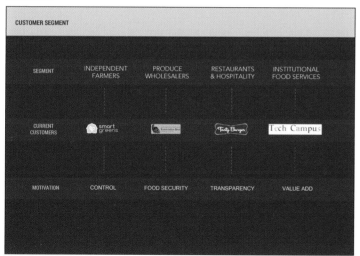

CUSTOMER SEGMENT				
SEGMENT	INDEPENDENT FARMERS	PRODUCE WHOLESALERS	RESTAURANTS & HOSPITALITY	INSTITUTIONAL FOOD SERVICES
CURRENT CUSTOMERS	smart greens		Tasty Burger	Tech Campus
MOTIVATION	CONTROL	FOOD SECURITY	TRANSPARENCY	VALUE ADD

Market

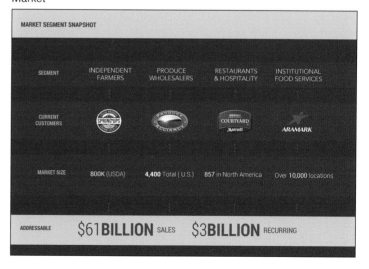

MARKET SEGMENT SNAPSHOT				
SEGMENT	INDEPENDENT FARMERS	PRODUCE WHOLESALERS	RESTAURANTS & HOSPITALITY	INSTITUTIONAL FOOD SERVICES
CURRENT CUSTOMERS	SPRING-UPS	PRODUCE ALLIANCE	COURTYARD Marriott	ARAMARK
MARKET SIZE	800K (USDA)	4,400 Total (U.S.)	857 in North America	Over 10,000 locations
ADDRESSABLE	**$61 BILLION** SALES	**$3 BILLION** RECURRING		

Hinge · **The dating and relationship app for young professionals.**

Founding team: Justin McLeod
Location: New York City
Funding round: Series seed
Market category: dating and social discovery

Founded by Justin McLeod, Hinge is the dating app for relationships, which works by introducing users to friends of friends. Hinge's deck opens by arguing for why mobile dating apps would be increasingly popular. We like the way Hinge goes beyond basic user numbers to show traction and focuses on visualizing their most important metrics: frequency of use and retention over time.

Common Mistakes Founders Make

"Entrepreneurs are often too willing to talk to any investor, which is not only a waste of time, but worse, it shifts the power dynamic in favor of the investor. Investing is like dating; it works better when your partner feels lucky to have you."

Advice

"No matter the stage, entrepreneurs should narrow the field, make the deal seem exclusive, and make investors feel that they are being chosen not just because they're the only ones willing to fund."

Redo

"I would have sold more of a vision up front about what we believed the dating app market would look like. This was mid-2013, before dating apps were popular. A better case could have been made that most single people would be using dating apps by 2015."

Slide Investors Focused on Most

"Investors spent the most time challenging the size of the market, both in terms of number of people and in terms of dollars, given that 'Match had already saturated the market.' Our belief was that the market would be an order of magnitude larger than it was in 2013, and that Match would NOT be the prime player."

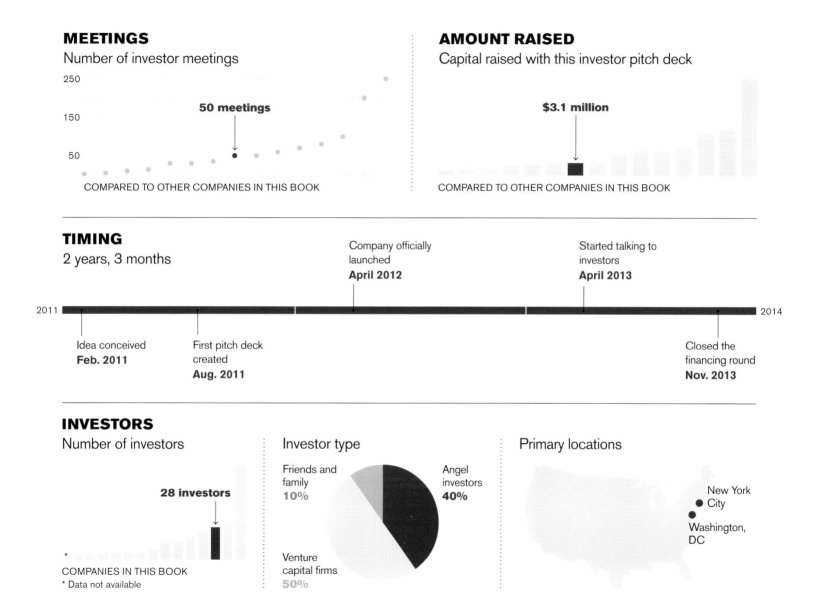

MEETINGS
Number of investor meetings

250

150

50

50 meetings

COMPARED TO OTHER COMPANIES IN THIS BOOK

AMOUNT RAISED
Capital raised with this investor pitch deck

$3.1 million

COMPARED TO OTHER COMPANIES IN THIS BOOK

TIMING
2 years, 3 months

2011

2014

Idea conceived
Feb. 2011

First pitch deck
created
Aug. 2011

Company officially
launched
April 2012

Started talking to
investors
April 2013

Closed the
financing round
Nov. 2013

INVESTORS
Number of investors

28 investors

*

COMPANIES IN THIS BOOK
* Data not available

Investor type

Friends and
family
10%

Angel
investors
40%

Venture
capital firms
50%

Primary locations

New York
City

Washington,
DC

Cover

History

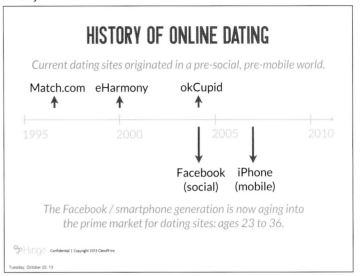

Problem

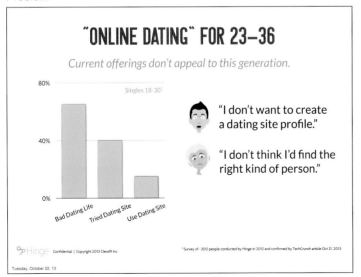

Solution

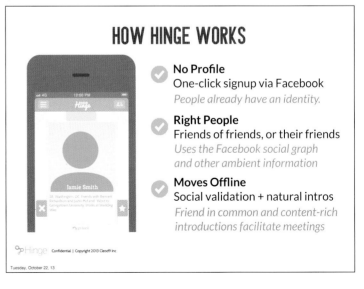

Traction

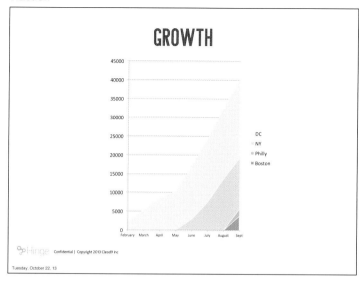

Market

Competition

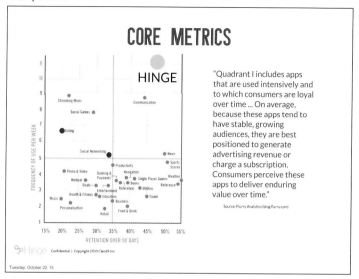

Product

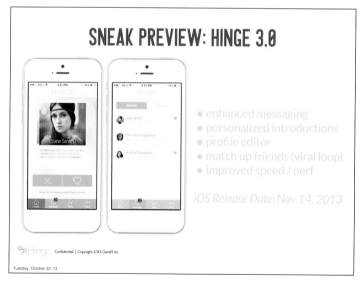

Karma · Get online easier than ever before by bringing Wi-Fi with you, everywhere you go.

Founding team: Stefan Borsje, Steven van Wel, Robert Gaal
Location: New York City
Market category: internet service providers; telecommunications; mobile

In early 2012 on a trip to New York, Steven van Wel was talking about Karma over lunch with a friend. Suddenly, this crazy guy walks up, tells him "hi," and walks off. A few hours later, Steven got an e-mail from David Tisch, at the time, the managing director of Techstars NYC. "You don't know me," David wrote, "But I just met you and you should move out to New York to join Techstars." That was the start of Karma's fundraising journey. Karma's deck does a lot in a small amount of real estate. Consistent formatting (big title at the top, main visual and content in the middle, and extra data at the bottom) keeps the deck clean and easy to digest.

Common Mistakes Founders Make

"A commitment isn't closing. Till the money is in . . . keep pitching. Maybe always means NO."

Advice

"Always follow up after every meeting. Send out weekly updates to everyone you've met with."

MEETINGS

Number of investor meetings

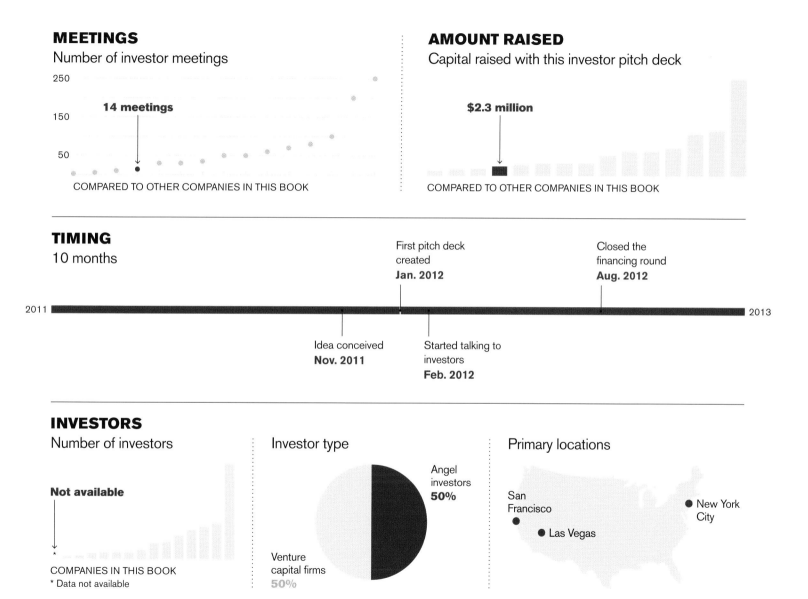

250

14 meetings

150

50

COMPARED TO OTHER COMPANIES IN THIS BOOK

AMOUNT RAISED

Capital raised with this investor pitch deck

$2.3 million

COMPARED TO OTHER COMPANIES IN THIS BOOK

TIMING

10 months

First pitch deck
created
Jan. 2012

Closed the
financing round
Aug. 2012

2011

2013

Idea conceived
Nov. 2011

Started talking to
investors
Feb. 2012

INVESTORS

Number of investors

Not available

*

COMPANIES IN THIS BOOK
* Data not available

Investor type

Angel
investors
50%

Venture
capital firms
50%

Primary locations

San
Francisco

Las Vegas

New York
City

Cover

Overview

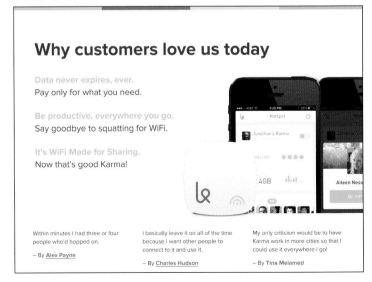

How It Works

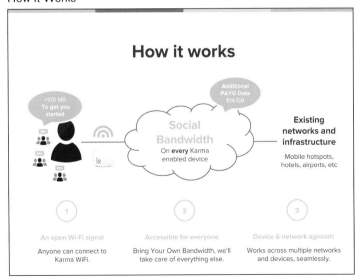

Customer Quotes

Traction

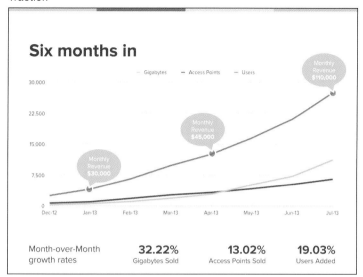

Solution

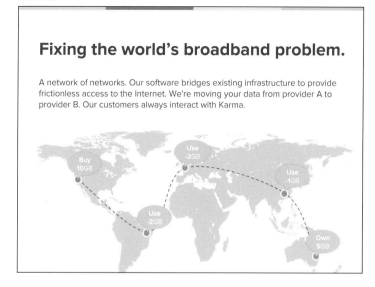

Go-to-Market Strategy

Team

Man Crates · Bragworthy gifts for men.

Founding team: Jonathan Beekman, Sam Gong
Location: Redwood, CA
Funding round: Series seed
Market category: e-commerce

Man Crates is a beautiful example of the power of brand and customer experience. Out of what would seem like an overcrowded space—online gift-giving—cofounder Jonathan Beekman has built a massively profitable business by focusing on building experiences people love. We like the "Customer Satisfaction" slide in particular. It shows Man Crates's Net Promoter Score stacked side-by-side with some of the world's most well-known brands.

Common Mistakes Founders Make

"It's very easy to waste time answering questions from investors who aren't really all that interested in investing. Some investors would rather get a free option on investing than just say no. You should push for a yes, but absent that, push for a no. Ignore anyone who says "maybe" without giving you specifics on when they'll make their decision; for the most part, these investors are a waste of time. Focus on those who have yet to say yes or no."

Advice

"Once you decide to start raising, focus on nothing else. It's tempting to devote ten hours a week to fundraising, but it's more like an eighty-hour-a-week full-time job. The faster you close, the faster you can get back to building your business. So plan to be fundraising for twice as long as you think it'll take, and if you close before then, consider yourself lucky."

Redo

"I'd spend a bit more time on the formatting and polish. I nearly always present this deck in person, so as a stand-alone document, it's not as useful as it could be. Before sending to investors, I'd trim a few of the slides so the deck was more of a teaser intro to help facilitate a face-to-face meeting."

Slide Investors Focused on Most

The financial slide.

MEETINGS

Number of investor meetings

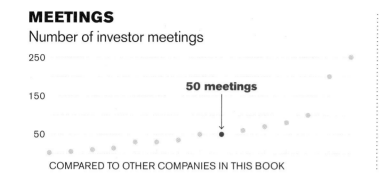

50 meetings

250

150

50

COMPARED TO OTHER COMPANIES IN THIS BOOK

AMOUNT RAISED

Capital raised with this investor pitch deck

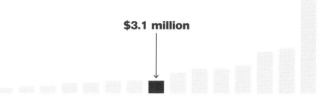

$3.1 million

COMPARED TO OTHER COMPANIES IN THIS BOOK

TIMING

3 years, 3 months

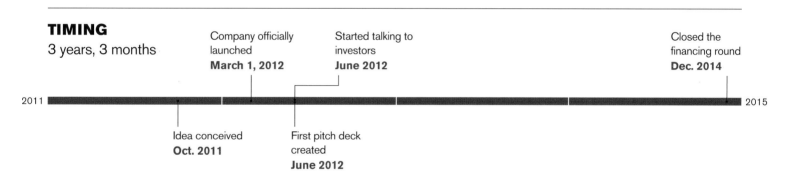

Company officially
launched
March 1, 2012

Started talking to
investors
June 2012

Closed the
financing round
Dec. 2014

2011

2015

Idea conceived
Oct. 2011

First pitch deck
created
June 2012

INVESTORS

Number of investors

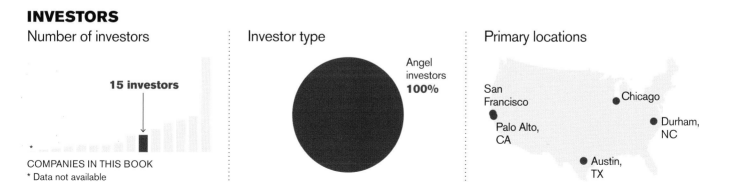

15 investors

COMPANIES IN THIS BOOK
* Data not available

Investor type

Angel
investors
100%

Primary locations

San
Francisco

Palo Alto,
CA

Chicago

Durham,
NC

Austin,
TX

Cover

Vision

Market

Problem

Solution

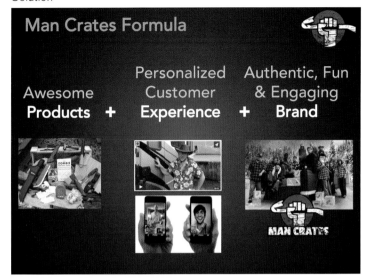

Screenshot

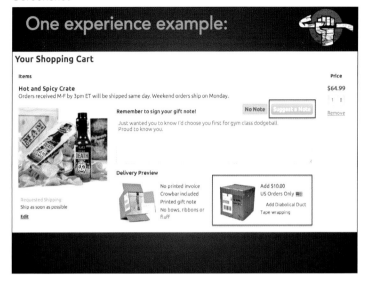

Core Metric

Customer

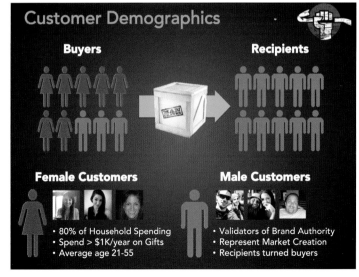

Reaction, Inc. • Designs and manufactures humanitarian-focused products.

Founding team: Michael McDaniel
Location: Austin, TX
Funding round: Series seed
Market category: Clean technology; hardware and software

Reaction is a design-centered venture, and their deck reflects that. What could be thought of a sleepy industry ("temporary housing") is made fascinating by a big idea communicated through beautiful design and compelling market data. All physical product companies should emulate their excellent use of product photography in this deck. Moreover, Reaction's social mission comes through subtly but strongly.

Common Mistakes Founders Make

"(1) Not telling a compelling story with a long-term vision. Create a company with a future; (2) Not doing dry or practice runs of their pitches before going on the road; (3) Wasting time with pitch competitions or pitching to the wrong audiences in general."

Advice

"There are lots of creative ways to raise funds these days, so make sure that venture capital is the right funding vehicle for your needs. You are selling off a part of your company, your dream, and your work, and introducing a lot of new voices in exchange for capital. Only go down this route as a method of last resort or with the certainty that a raise will get your company where it needs to be. Then raise only what you need and at a valuation that you can live with forever. Remember, fundraising is not the end game; it is just the beginning."

Redo

"I would add a product road map slide to show the vision and ambition of the company over a seven- or even a ten-year time span. This one slide would have told investors that we are not a flash in the pan or that we would not get bored with things sixteen months in."

Slide Investors Focused on Most

"Competitive landscape."

MEETINGS

Number of investor meetings

250 meetings

250

150

50

COMPARED TO OTHER COMPANIES IN THIS BOOK

AMOUNT RAISED

Capital raised with this investor pitch deck

$1.5 million

COMPARED TO OTHER COMPANIES IN THIS BOOK

TIMING

8 years, 8 months

Started talking to investors
Aug. 2013

Company officially launched
March 2014

2005

2015

Idea conceived
Aug. 2005

First pitch deck created
April 2007

Closed the financing round
Jan. 2014

INVESTORS

Number of investors

31 investors

*
COMPANIES IN THIS BOOK
* Data not available

Investor type

Accelerators
0.4%

Angel investors
64%

Venture capital firms
36%

Primary locations

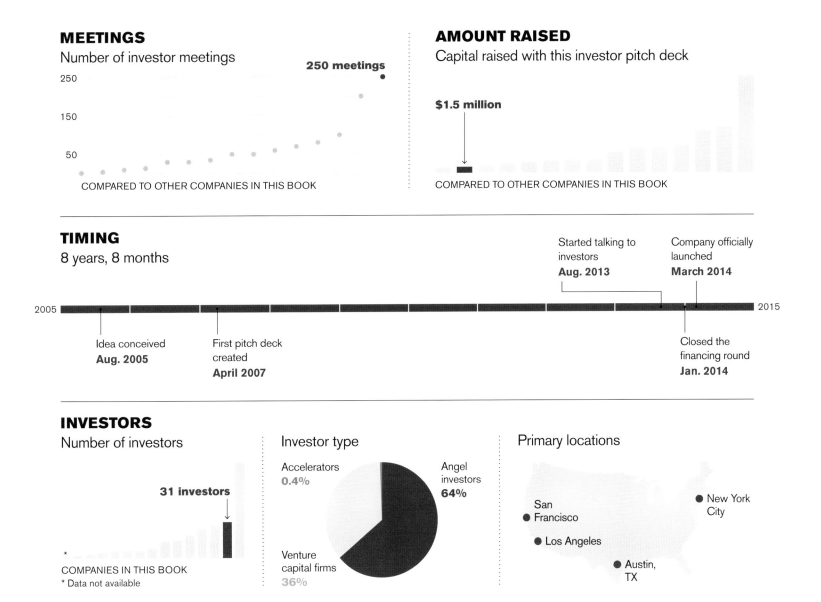

San Francisco

● New York City

● Los Angeles

● Austin, TX

Cover

Overview

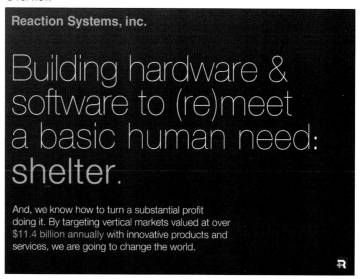

Reaction Systems, inc.

Building hardware & software to (re)meet a basic human need: shelter.

And, we know how to turn a substantial profit doing it. By targeting vertical markets valued at over $11.4 billion annually with innovative products and services, we are going to change the world.

Problem

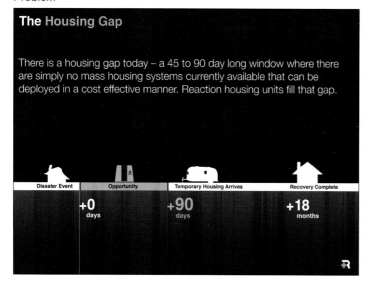

The Housing Gap

There is a housing gap today – a 45 to 90 day long window where there are simply no mass housing systems currently available that can be deployed in a cost effective manner. Reaction housing units fill that gap.

Disaster Event	Opportunity	Temporary Housing Arrives	Recovery Complete
+0 days	+90 days		+18 months

Solution

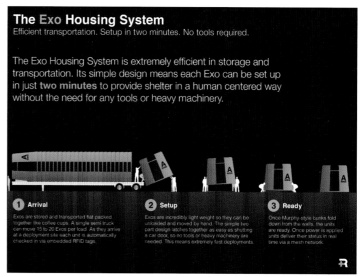

The Exo Housing System

Efficient transportation. Setup in two minutes. No tools required.

The Exo Housing System is extremely efficient in storage and transportation. Its simple design means each Exo can be set up in just **two minutes** to provide shelter in a human centered way without the need for any tools or heavy machinery.

1 Arrival
Exos are stored and transported flat packed together like coffee cups. A single semi truck can move 15 to 20 Exos per load. As they arrive at a deployment site each unit is automatically checked in via embedded RFID tags.

2 Setup
Exos are incredibly light weight so they can be unloaded and moved by hand. The simple two part design latches together as easy as shutting a car door, so no tools or heavy machinery are needed. This means extremely fast deployments.

3 Ready
Once Murphy-style bunks fold down from the walls, the units are ready. Once power is applied units deliver their status in real time via a mesh network.

Product

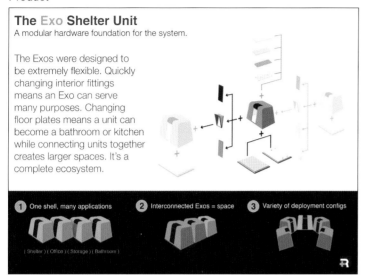

The Exo Shelter Unit
A modular hardware foundation for the system.

The Exos were designed to be extremely flexible. Quickly changing interior fittings means an Exo can serve many purposes. Changing floor plates means a unit can become a bathroom or kitchen while connecting units together creates larger spaces. It's a complete ecosystem.

1. One shell, many applications
(Shelter) (Office) (Storage) (Bathroom)

2. Interconnected Exos = space

3. Variety of deployment configs

Competition

Competitive Landscape
Our closest, existing competitors

Despite a tremendous TAM, at present there are no direct competitors in market. Here are the closest competitors by type.

MIL. SPEC TENTS	MODIFIED CONTAINERS	TRAVEL TRAILERS	PREFAB STRUCTURES
• Inexpensive	• Cheap materials	• Kitchen & restroom	• Good for long durations
• Very portable	• Mass shipping friendly	• "Trailer Park" feel	• Kitchen & restroom
• No privacy	• Lots of hand fabrication	• Low volume transport	• Long lead times
• Not secure	• Needs heavy machinery	• Expensive hookups	• Low volume transport
Competitors:	Competitors:	Competitors:	Competitors:
Eureka!	Global Portable	Gulfstream Coach	Clayton Homes
Mahaffey	Industrial Crewquarters	Keystone	Action Mobile Industries
HDT Global	Aztec Container	Forest River	Pacific Mobile
$3,600 +	$16,390 +	$18,000 +	$26,000 +

Go-to-Market Strategy

Go to Market Strategy
Focus on three vertical markets provides stable & diverse cash flow

We will generate a steady cash flow through direct sales and support of the Exo Housing System components to three vertical markets.

1. FIELD SERVICES
Science research stations; Military; Utilities & Construction base camps

Sales Cycle: Short | Medium | Long

Example Customers:
NASA
Variety of agencies and universities
U.S. Military
Foreign Militaries
Various Site Operators

Worth over $3.2b annually

2. RECREATIONAL
Large scale multi-day music & sporting events; camping & hunting

Sales Cycle: Short | Medium | Long

Example Customers:
SXSW / ACL / Coachella
Large Event Organizers
Cabela's / REI / Other "Outfitters"
Wal-Mart (Outfitter)
City & County Governments

Worth over $156m annually

3. DISASTER RESPONSE
Government agencies & suppliers; small to large NGO's

Sales Cycle: Short | Medium | Long

Example Customers:
FEMA's Suppliers
United Nations
Red Cross
Foreign Governments
Variety of small & large NGOs

Worth over $8.1b annually

Team

The Reaction Team

CORE TEAM

MICHAEL MCDANIEL
Founder & CEO
A proven systematic thinker with numerous appearances at TED, Michael has led large, diverse teams to solve complex problems for a variety of Fortune 100 clients for over 13 years. His broad skill set and thoughtful approach to design have created effective solutions for clients including MTV, Comcast, AT&T, American Airlines, HP, Skype, Honeywell, and Disney among others.

GRAEME WAITZKIN
COO
Graeme brings a unique combination of strategy, design, engineering, and entrepreneurial leadership. As a strategy director at frog and IDEO, Graeme helped industrial giants like GE build new, design-led businesses. Previously, Graeme led the development of award-winning, DoD certified devices for homeland security. Graeme holds an MBA and MS from Stanford, and degrees in Structural Engineering and Engineering Management from Duke.

THOMAS BRADY
Technology
Thomas is a design technologist who "sketches" with code and a soldering iron. He has worked across the entire spectrum of technology development and implementation from courseware delivery platforms for Harvard Business School to next generation products for Polycom and S&P to crowd generated data visualizations at frog.

OUR ADVISORY BOARD

DOREEN LORENZO
Doreen is the president of Quirky.com. Prior to Quirky, she was the president of frog and an executive vice president/general manager of Aricent. During her almost 17 years with frog, she was instrumental in re-structuring the company, taking it from a traditional, small design boutique to one of the world's foremost global innovation firms all while growing revenue over 1000%.

KIP THOMPSON
As Vice President at Dell, Kip was responsible for overseeing 16 million square feet of manufacturing, and facilities in 130 locations worldwide. He spearheaded Dell's expansion into emerging markets in Asia, Europe, the Middle East, Latin America and Africa. He built manufacturing facilities and opened offices all over the world. Kip is not just an advisor at Reaction, but also an investor.

PIVOT
Pivot is a partnership of some of the most successful and seasoned professionals in product design, venture capital and entrepreneurship. This amazing accelerator and investor group is very passionate about Reaction's mission providing advisement and mentorship across several key areas. Given their current positions and existing relationships we can not disclose their names.

Shift • Takes care of every step in buying or selling a car.
Better deals, real advice, and free on-demand test drives or appraisals.

Founding team: George Arison, Christian Ohler, Minnie Ingersoll, Joel Washington, Morgan Knutson
Location: Santa Monica, CA
Funding round: Series A
Market category: technology

Shift's deck opens with a description of each founding team member's accomplishments—one of Shift's key strengths. The minimalist design reinforces their mission to simplify a complex and broken process. We love their use of full-bleed imagery and focus on showing the product. Finally, the photography of the filled car garage—the "hub"—reminds that reader that this is not merely a vision—it is live.

Common Mistakes Founders Make
"(1) Lots of CEOs think that valuation drives how much you raise. In reality, it's how much you raise that drives the valuation; (2) Optimize for raising more money than you need; do not optimize for dilution. At an early stage, raise thinking that you will have no revenue for eighteen to twenty-four months; (3) Don't focus on the funds, focus on partners at those funds; what matters is who you are working with day to day."

Advice
"Focus on the people you will be working with, more than any other optimization. In my view, the team is the most important and awesome thing about Shift. I have incredible cofounders, both technical and operational, without whom none of this would have been possible. The biggest thing is team. Bring onboard awesome team members, before you do anything else."

Redo
"I was actually pretty happy with the deck, so not much to change, especially since the final version has some edits from VC feedback."

Slide Investors Focused on Most
"Team and product vision."

MEETINGS

Number of investor meetings

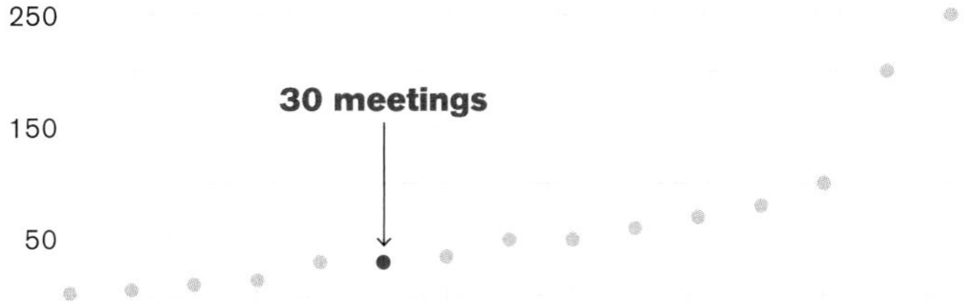

250

30 meetings

150

50

COMPARED TO OTHER COMPANIES IN THIS BOOK

AMOUNT RAISED

Capital raised with this investor pitch deck

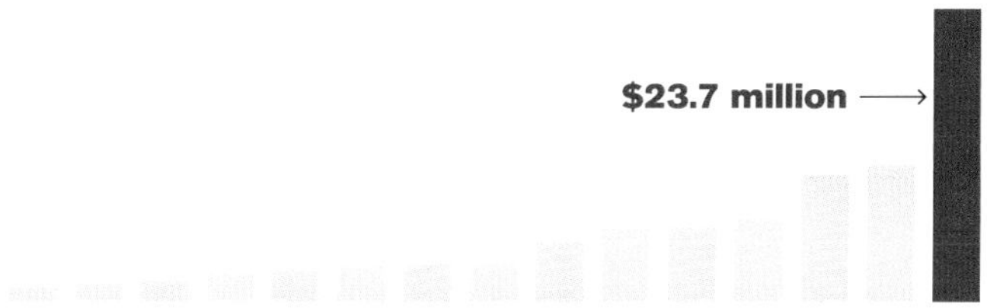

$23.7 million →

COMPARED TO OTHER COMPANIES IN THIS BOOK

TIMING

3 years, 6 months

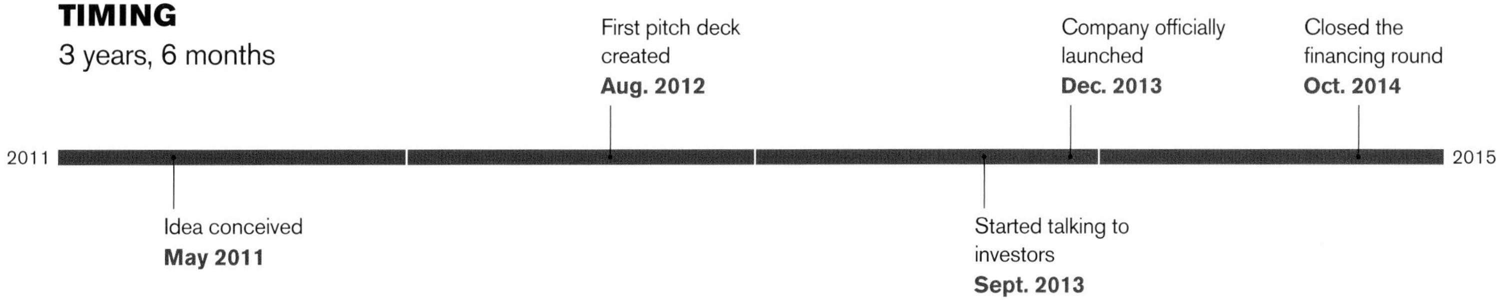

First pitch deck
created
Aug. 2012

Company officially
launched
Dec. 2013

Closed the
financing round
Oct. 2014

2011

2015

Idea conceived
May 2011

Started talking to
investors
Sept. 2013

INVESTORS

Number of investors

82 investors →

*

COMPANIES IN THIS BOOK
* Data not available

Investor type

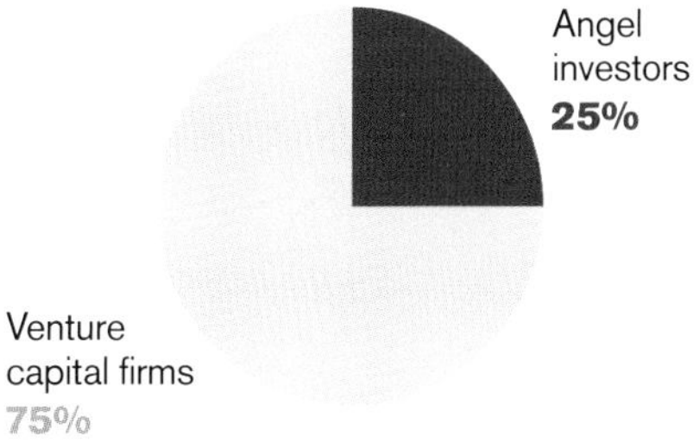

Angel
investors
25%

Venture
capital firms
75%

Primary locations

New York
● City

● San
Francisco

Washington,
DC

Cover

Team

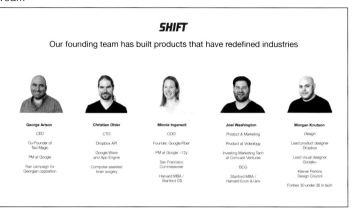

Market

Problem

Solution

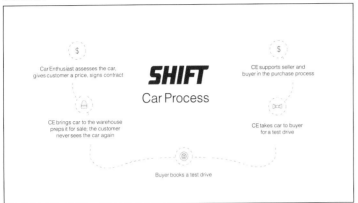

Product

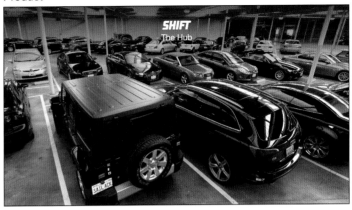

Screenshot

Screenshot

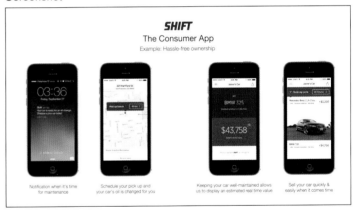

SOLS Systems · Dynamic, custom insoles engineered to change the way you move.

Founding team: Kegan Schouwenburg, Joel Wish
Location: New York City
Funding round: Series B
Market category: medical devices; fashion; 3D printing

SOLS is an orthotics startup with a big vision: to revolutionize manufacturing. The deck is beautiful. We love their use of imagery and negative space. Succinct, provocative copy fills the center of the slides. We also like how they use darkened images or faded images to fill the background.

Common Mistakes Founders Make

"Being self-critical. Raise the right amount of money for what you want to achieve. Too much, too soon can be just as bad as too little, too late. Not realizing that 'maybe' almost always means no."

Advice

"Early-stage investing isn't rational. It's a mix of market trends, relationships, adrenaline, and appetite for risk. No matter how good your hockey stick looks, no one knows if your startup will succeed or fail. Get comfortable being uncomfortable, and take people on the journey. If you're doing your job, your startup will outpace you. It's OK. This doesn't mean you're getting fired. No one expects you to know every job, but they do expect you to hire people who can. Doing this well will make or break your company, your schedule, your culture, and ultimately, your success. No pressure. Do the best you can today, and do better tomorrow."

Redo

"My approach to forecasting, focusing more narrowly on key performance indicators and less on vanity metrics and hockey-stick growth. Market aside, a startup's trajectory is a direct reflection of the levers you pull, how hard you pull them, and in what order."

Slide Investors Focused on Most

"Most often we talked through the deck without actually focusing or even looking at the slides. Very rarely did I find myself pitching in the traditional sense."

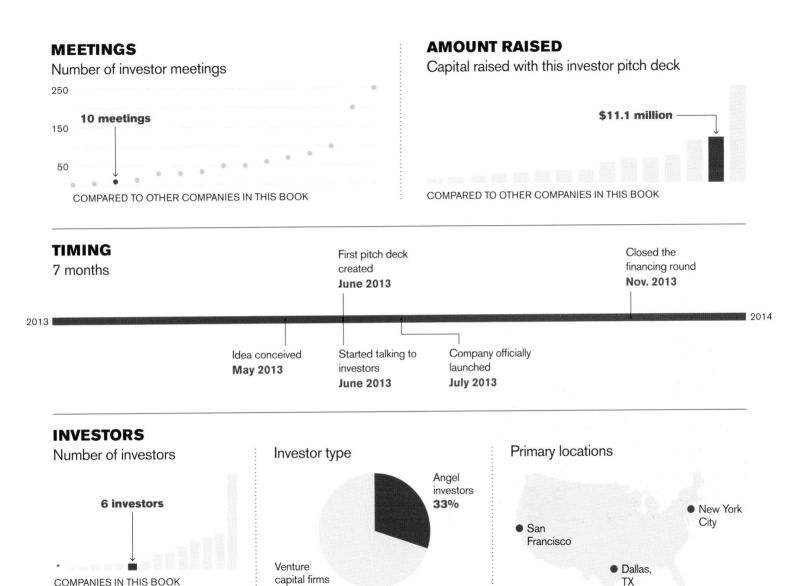

MEETINGS
Number of investor meetings

250

10 meetings

150

50

COMPARED TO OTHER COMPANIES IN THIS BOOK

AMOUNT RAISED
Capital raised with this investor pitch deck

$11.1 million

COMPARED TO OTHER COMPANIES IN THIS BOOK

TIMING
7 months

2013

First pitch deck
created
June 2013

Closed the
financing round
Nov. 2013

2014

Idea conceived
May 2013

Started talking to
investors
June 2013

Company officially
launched
July 2013

INVESTORS
Number of investors

6 investors

*

COMPANIES IN THIS BOOK
* Data not available

Investor type

Angel
investors
33%

Venture
capital firms
67%

Primary locations

San
Francisco

New York
City

Dallas,
TX

Cover

SOLS

Overview

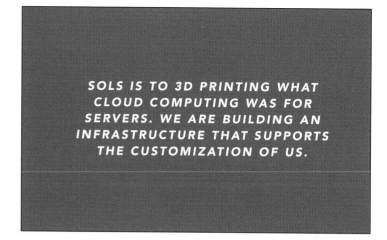
SOLS IS TO 3D PRINTING WHAT CLOUD COMPUTING WAS FOR SERVERS. WE ARE BUILDING AN INFRASTRUCTURE THAT SUPPORTS THE CUSTOMIZATION OF US.

Solution

PRODUCT AS A SERVICE

Our vertically integrated hardware as software model leverages digital manufacturing + design to enable rapid development of physical goods

Want to sell SOLS? Get our software.

Minimal set-up costs
Extensive customization
Rapid iteration
Zero inventory
Subscription vs. one-time transaction

Market

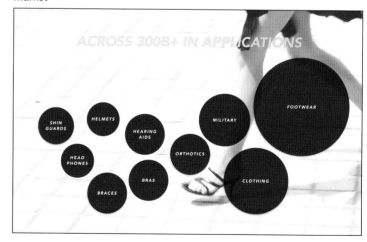
ACROSS 300B+ IN APPLICATIONS

SHIN GUARDS
HELMETS
HEARING AIDS
MILITARY
FOOTWEAR
HEAD PHONES
ORTHOTICS
BRACES
BRAS
CLOTHING

Solution

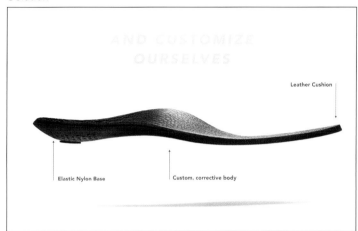

Opportunity

Customer Quote

Vision

Tegu · Tegu is a magnetic wooden alternative to LEGO.

Founding team: Will and Chris Haughey
Location: Darien, CT
Funding round: Series B
Market category: toys

Tegu is a toy company with a powerful story. Founders Will and Chris Haughey created Tegu to be a socially driven company, focusing on job creation for the poor in Honduras while also building a profitable business. As a result, they attracted a certain profile of investor who both believed in their mission and the investment opportunity. Like their magnetic wooden blocks, the Tegu deck strikes a perfect balance of beauty and utility.

Common Mistakes Founders Make

They spend too much time preparing information. In the end, people invest in concepts and people that they trust. It's also easy to waste time with prospects who don't really have experience in investments of your risk profile.

Advice

Your goal is to get the person across the table to conclude for themselves "this could be huge." After that, it's just the details of how much they'll commit. Plan for delays and always be closing. Time kills deals.

Redo

I would add a Use of Proceeds slide. I'd probably also add a more robust competitive positioning slide so outsiders to the industry could understand it quickly.

Slide Investors Focused on Most

Investors don't spend much time on slides, but if I had to pick, it would be the financials. Investors often asked, "So, how does this thing make money?"

MEETINGS

Number of investor meetings

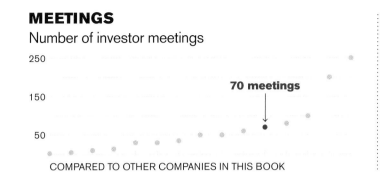

70 meetings

COMPARED TO OTHER COMPANIES IN THIS BOOK

AMOUNT RAISED

Capital raised with this investor pitch deck

$5 million

COMPARED TO OTHER COMPANIES IN THIS BOOK

TIMING

7 years, 8 months

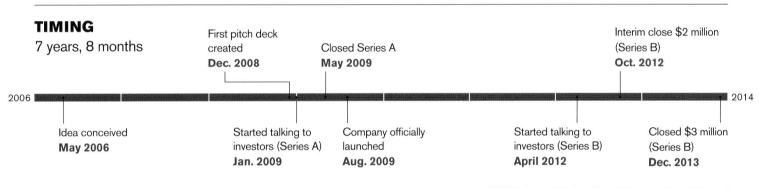

First pitch deck
created
Dec. 2008

Closed Series A
May 2009

Interim close $2 million
(Series B)
Oct. 2012

2006

2014

Idea conceived
May 2006

Started talking to
investors (Series A)
Jan. 2009

Company officially
launched
Aug. 2009

Started talking to
investors (Series B)
April 2012

Closed $3 million
(Series B)
Dec. 2013

INVESTORS

Number of investors

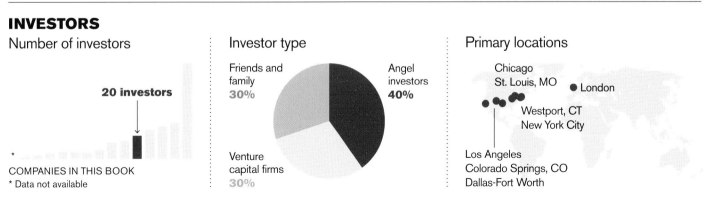

20 investors

*

COMPANIES IN THIS BOOK
* Data not available

Investor type

Friends and
family
30%

Angel
investors
40%

Venture
capital firms
30%

Primary locations

Chicago
St. Louis, MO ● London

Westport, CT
New York City

Los Angeles
Colorado Springs, CO
Dallas-Fort Worth

Cover

tegu

Investment Overview

Company Overview

Tegu is building the world's most innovative premium toy company. Better research. Better design. And, a modern brand to boot.

Company History

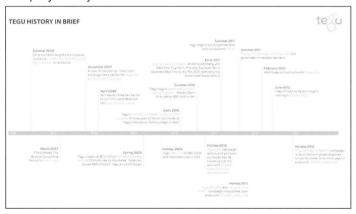

Opportunity

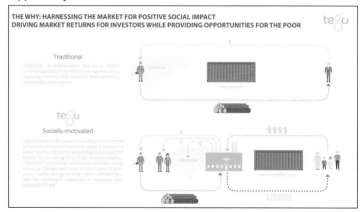

Milestones

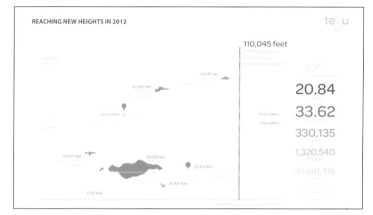

Sales

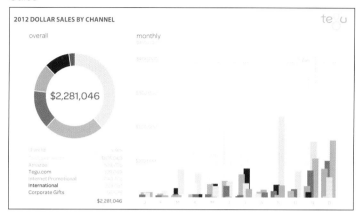

Press

Financials

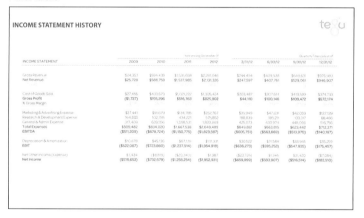

TreeHouse · Category-redefining home improvement company focused on home design and performance.

Founding team: Evan Loomis, Jason Ballard, Kevin Graham, Paul Yanosy, Pete Ackerson, and Brian Williamson
Location: Austin, TX
Funding round: Series A
Market category: home improvement; sustainability

The Whole Foods version of Home Depot. That was the original pitch for TreeHouse when Loomis and his co-founders were getting the venture off the ground. The deck focuses on building the case for why residential and commercial building is the next green revolution, and why TreeHouse is the team to pull it off.

Common Mistakes Founders Make
"Successful entrepreneurs raise friends first, not cash. To say it another way, successful entrepreneurs don't raise cash at the expense of friendship. I've seen a lot of entrepreneurs lose friendships, trust, and momentum because they get this fundamental truth mixed up."

Advice
"Read this book."

Redo
"We incorporated a lot of full-bleed imagery in our later investor presentations. I think pictures do a better job of capturing people's imaginations faster. One point of consistent feedback with this presentation was to 'get to the product' faster. We had dedicated our first ten slides to 'trends,' 'opportunity,' and the 'industry overview.' Investors got a little bored with the slow buildup."

Slide Investors Focused on Most
"Three slides dominated most of the conversation: (1) The trends slide titled 'Someone will do this' generated most of the feedback from investors. It was easy to understand since we stacked logos in the respective industry verticals; (2) The opportunity slide titled 'Elements of a green home are everywhere' came in second. Investors felt that this was a futuristic sneak peek into the future of home building; (3) The solution slide with the TreeHouse storefront generated lots of conversation as well. You could immediately tell if investors appreciated the concept on this slide. They would either say 'cool' or shrug their shoulders in indifference."

MEETINGS

Number of investor meetings

250

150

200 meetings ●

50

COMPARED TO OTHER COMPANIES IN THIS BOOK

AMOUNT RAISED

Capital raised with this investor pitch deck

$6.75 million

↓

COMPARED TO OTHER COMPANIES IN THIS BOOK

TIMING

5 years, 9 months

First pitch deck
created
May 2009

Closed the
financing round
Feb. 2011

2006 ————————————————————————————————— 2012

Idea conceived
Feb. 2006

Evan Loomis left job,
bootstrapped, and built
team and partners
Feb. 2009

Started talking to
investors
Sept. 2009

Company officially
launched
Oct. 2011

INVESTORS

Number of investors

25 investors

↓

*

COMPANIES IN THIS BOOK
* Data not available

Investor type

Friends and
family
25%

Angel
investors
65%

Venture
capital firms
10%

Primary locations

New York
City

Washington,
DC

Austin,
Dallas,
San Antonio,
TX

Hong
Kong

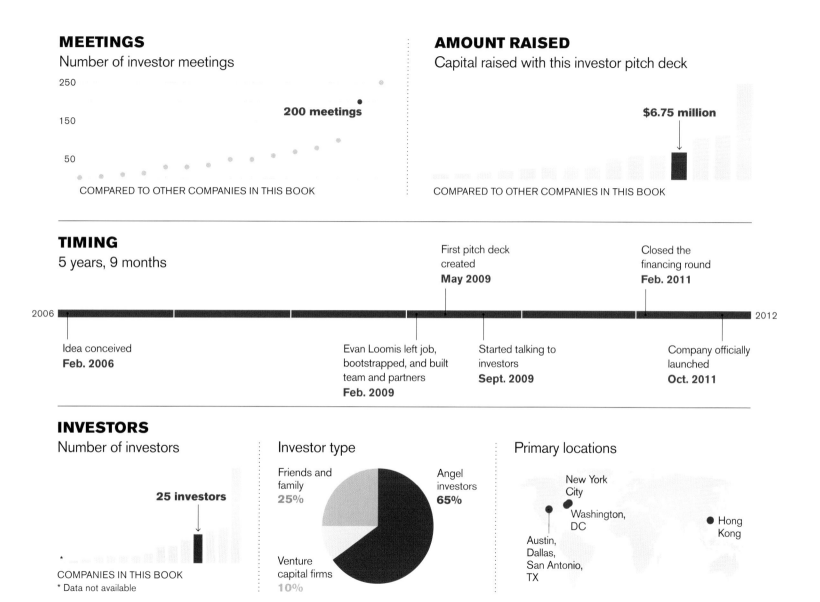

Cover

Opportunity

Opportunity

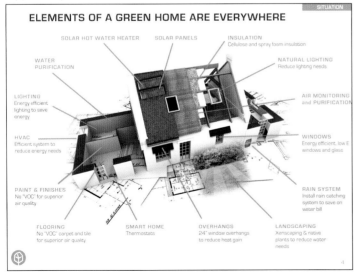

Market

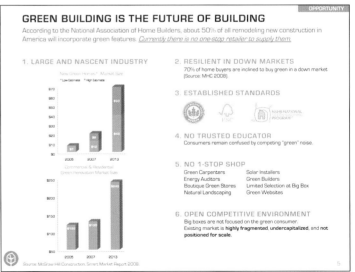

Solution

Growth Plans

Partners

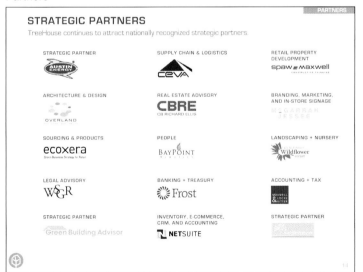

Investment Highlights

7

Pitching Exercises

This chapter brings together the best in experiential learning on pitching. It outlines several exercises—some easy, some bizarre—that entrepreneurs have used to turn their mediocre pitching into confident, powerful, cash-earning pitches. The goal with each of these exercises is to build your pitch muscle, to help you get over yourself, to become more comfortable telling your story, and to identify the style of pitching that resonates for your particular venture and personality.

Be warned, many of these exercises will feel awkward. Embrace the awkwardness. These exercises are what the best of the best use to teach the art of pitching.

Pitching Exercises:

- The Techstars Jedi Mind Trick

- The d.school Pitch Frameworks

- The Dry Run

- The Spy Dry Run

The Techstars Jedi Mind Trick

From Jason Seats, Partner at Techstars

How long does it take? Five minutes

Who do you need? You and one person who doesn't know anything about your venture

You've got twenty words. With those words, can you get someone to ask you the question you want to be asked about your venture?

To play the game, find someone who knows nothing about your venture to play with you. Then, tell the person your elevator pitch. As soon as you are done, ask the person, "What's the first question that comes to your mind?"

You may be surprised by what you hear. Jason talks about his experience playing this game with Techstars companies:

> The entrepreneurs may not know what question they wanted them to ask, but they sure know that wasn't it. "That question tells me they think we're in a completely different industry." It's about leaving the right holes, leaving an obvious gap for the other participant in the conversation to step into.

In the words of East Coast investor Walt Winshall, "Don't steal their line."

> *Entrepreneur:* "I'm going to tell you the elevator pitch of the venture I'm working on, and afterward I want you to ask me the first question that pops into your head. Sound good?"
>
> *Listener:* "I guess so."
>
> [Entrepreneur gives pitch.]
>
> [Listener asks the first question that comes to him.]

Afterward, reflect on the following:

1. Was that the question you expected to hear? What did you want to hear?

2. What does that question tell you about what the listener understands about your venture?

3. What changes can you make to your pitch to set up the kind of conversation you want to have?

The d.school Pitch Frameworks

From the LaunchPad, d.school, Stanford University

How long does it take? Thirty minutes

Who do you need? Just you

With the bold claim of being able to take startup founders from idea to revenue in ten weeks, the LaunchPad program at the Institute of Design at Stanford University (known as the d.school) is a perfect place to search for transformative experiences. And when it comes to pitching, the school doesn't disappoint. One of the key philosophies of the d.school is to use forms of play to overcome fear and unleash creativity. If you are having trouble telling your story in a unique way, or if you get gripped by a sinking feeling whenever you think about giving your pitch, this exercise is for you. Here are eight pitch frameworks, playful ways to tell and retell your pitch.

For each framework, we use the example of Loomis's venture, TreeHouse, to show you how it works.

1. The One-Word Pitch

If you could only use one word to describe what you want others to know, do, and feel about your venture, what would it be?

Green-building

2. The Pixar Pitch

Originally presented by Pixar storyboard artist Emma Coats, this framework fits every single Pixar movie made and, arguably, every story ever made.

Once upon a time there was ———————.

Every day, ————————————.

One day ——————————————.

Because of that, ———————————.

Because of that, ———————————.

Until finally ————————————.

Once upon a time, there was a thriving industry for do-it-yourself home improvement.

Every day, homeowners and contractors used stores like Home Depot and Lowe's to renovate and maintain their homes.

One day, people began to become more conscious of their environmental impact.

Because of that, they began to seek out sustainable alternatives for things they were already buying. For food, they went to Whole Foods. For clothes, they shopped at stores like Patagonia.

Because of that, people began to look for sustainable alternatives for home improvement.

Until finally, TreeHouse created the first sustainable home improvement store.

3. The Obituary Pitch

Morbid but powerful. Imagine it's seventy years from now. You just died. The *Wall Street Journal* opens your obituary describing your company and its legacy and contribution. What does it say?

When Evan left his job in investment banking, he had no idea that the venture he would help start would change the culture of the home-building industry in America. TreeHouse, the first sustainable home-improvement store, marked a shift in how Americans renovated and maintained their homes—eventually rivaling the big players in the industry, Home Depot and Lowe's. Today, in large part due to TreeHouse,

homeowners are more educated and empowered to build sustainably.

4. The Beaming Review Pitch

A customer just rated your product five stars on the App Store/Amazon/Yelp. What does the fifty-word blurb that she wrote say?

Bar none the best place to buy DIY. If Lowe's and Whole Foods had a baby, it would be TreeHouse. If you care about the environment, your family, or home improvement then you should consider stopping by. Don't trust me; come and see for yourself. You won't be disappointed.

5. The Proud Grandparent Pitch

What would your technologically illiterate grandma say if she were bragging about your company? Keep in mind, her bridge friends probably don't care about the technical details. What do they care about?

The people are so sweet and nice at TreeHouse! Just the most well-mannered and polite bunch of young folks you'll ever meet in your life.

6. The Three-Act Play in Three Sentences

Write a three-sentence pitch in the style of a three-act play.

ACT I: Introduce hero.

ACT II: Get hero in trouble.

ACT III: Get hero out of trouble.

ACT 1: You care about the environment. You care about your home. And you love DIY.

ACT 2: You just bought an old house. Uh-oh. There's so much to renovate, but how can you make sure what you buy matches your values?

ACT 3: That's when you discover TreeHouse, the first sustainable home improvement store. What a life saver!

7. The Haiku Pitch

Pitching your venture with seventeen syllables can be fun. Try it.

Green-building made fun
Education, great service
Smart home improvement

8. The Drunk Hemingway Pitch

The d.school team got this idea from the movie *Midnight in Paris*, in which a nostalgic writer finds himself on the streets of Paris in the twenties and runs into the Lost Generation—Hemingway, Fitzgerald, and a host of the other famous expatriates living in France at the time. In the movie, Hemingway talks about his work:

You liked my book? Yes, it was a good book because it was an honest book. And that's what war does to men. There's nothing fine and noble about dying in the mud. Unless you die gracefully. And then it's not only noble but brave.

(Google it.) Borrow the style for your pitch.

It is a good _____ because it is a _____ _____. There's nothing _____ and _____ about _____, unless you _____. And then, it's not only _____ but _____.

It is a good *home improvement store* because it is a *smart home improvement store*. There's nothing *fun* and *exciting* about *housework*, unless you *are building a home you love*. And then, it's not only *fun* but *beautiful*.

The Dry Run

How long does it take? Ten to thirty minutes

Who do you need? One to three friendly faces

There is no substitute for simply giving the pitch. No matter how many times you look through and revise your deck or talk through your pitch in your head, you won't really know how you perform in the field until you get out there and do it. Ask a few people who know and love you to fill in as your audience, and pitch just as you would to an investor. Ask one of them to video record you (just use a phone; no need to get fancy), so you can watch it afterward and debrief how it went. Once you start to pitch, give no prefaces or qualifications; don't break character. The more lifelike your practice is, the more comfortable you will be during the real thing. You will be surprised how many small details come up during the practice that you never would have thought of otherwise.

Here are a few possible variations on the dry run.

A Formal Pitch Presentation

Give the pitch as you would to a group of partners at a venture capital firm. Start the dry run from the moment you enter the building. Who do you first greet when you walk into the office? What do you say? How do you set up your laptop? Do you make small talk first or launch straight into the presentation? What happens when you are finished?

A Coffee Shop Pitch

Ask a friend to meet you for coffee so you can give her your pitch to play as if she were an angel investor you were meeting for the first time. Again, start the dry run from the moment you walk in the coffee shop. Are you early? How early? Who buys the coffee? What makes this experience different from a more formal pitch?

With the Deck/Without the Deck

You need to be prepared to give your presentation with and without the deck. Baehr once went to pitch a very wealthy man in Colorado; he arrived with his laptop and PDF ready to pitch and found himself sitting on an overstuffed leather couch in a room that resembled a country club. The investor walked in and said, "Tell me what you are working on." Even if you are meeting a venture capitalist at their office, they may have read the deck already and merely ask for a quick overview.

The Spy Dry Run

How long does it take? Thirty minutes

Who do you need? An angel/high-net-worth individual you know well

This exercise is designed specifically for accelerators and other entrepreneurship training and education organizations. Despite all the practice, it can still be very difficult to know how your entrepreneurs are doing in the real world. To get that kind of data, you'll need to ask an investor in your network to have a meeting with an entrepreneur solely for the purpose of seeing how he or she behaves. The entrepreneur shouldn't know that the meeting is a practice run—as far as he or she is concerned, this is as real as it gets. And, to be fair, it should be as real as it gets; the entrepreneur just doesn't know the investor is going to be debriefing with you afterward. Ask the investor to be as honest as possible in the critique. It is a good idea to do this with more than one investor, so you can overcome bias in any one investor and begin to see patterns.

Questions Investors Should Be Asking Themselves

- What is this person's body language like?

- Why would I not invest?

- What gets me excited about this opportunity?

GET
BACKED

Fundraising is a process of acquiring capital only in the most basic sense. In the truest sense, it is a process of finding a partner who is going to be with you through building a company for longer than many people are with their spouses.

—*Chi-Hua Chien, venture capitalist, Goodwater Capital, investor in Twitter, Facebook, and Spotify*

8

A Primer on Startup Financing

This chapter focuses on the basics of startup financing—the different mechanisms for raising money, the how and why of funding rounds, and the purpose of financing agreements. It's designed to give first-time founders an introduction to the language of financing, so you can move on to the much more difficult skill of building relationships. If phrases like "pre-money valuation" and "convertible note" scare the hell out of you, you are in the right place. Don't get too caught up in trying to understand the ins and outs of startup financing, though. Most of the investors we know are much more interested in finding entrepreneurs they believe in and want to work with than they are in negotiating the best possible deal.

Key Elements:

- The four ways to raise money
- How funding rounds work
- Understanding equity financing agreements

The Four Ways to Raise Money

At the most basic level, all ventures raise cash through one or more of these four mechanisms.

Create It through Profits

Creating cash through profits is what businesses are designed to do. Businesses are "value creating" machines, and cash is simply an agreed-upon amount of stored value. One option for getting the cash you need would be to use the venture itself, or another venture, to create cash through selling a product or service. In other words, you sell some products for more than it cost you to make them, then take the profit and use it to make and sell more products. You could also sell a service like consulting and use the profits from that service to build your business. People call this "bootstrapping." It is by far the cheapest form of getting cash. It can also be very slow. Many businesses finance their growth through this method.

Where does it come from?

- Revenues – Expenses = Profits

Borrow It through Debt

Borrowing cash is another word for debt. With debt, you pay someone a monthly "rental fee" called interest in exchange for access to their cash. However, institutions that lend cash like to have assurances that you are going to pay that cash back. They often require some sort of collateral, like a factory or a big piece of machinery, so that if you can't pay back the cash, they can take your factory instead and sell it to get the cash.

Borrowing cash through debt is more expensive than creating it, because you have to pay the interest (rental fee) each month, and it's also risky to you, because if you can't afford to pay back the money or the interest on time, the person who lent you money can bring you into bankruptcy.

Where does it come from?

- Investment banks
- Commercial banks
- Savings and loans
- Lending platforms like Able

Buy It through Selling Equity

Another way of raising money is to buy the cash by selling the most valuable thing you have: ownership of your venture and the future profits it might create. You hope your venture is going to be worth a lot of money, and anyone who owns a piece will have a claim to all that money. By selling equity to investors, you offer them a stake in the business—a percentage of ownership that you all agree on. Selling equity is typically thought of as the most expensive option for funding a venture, because if the venture does well, you end up giving away a bunch of money you could have had yourself. However, that's only if the venture would have been just as successful without selling that equity. If you have to move fast or if you have investors that bring more than just money, selling equity can be a key part of the business's success.

Where does it come from?

- Private equity

- Hedge funds

- Venture capital

- Angel investors

Get People to Donate It

There's one other way to raise money for your venture: ask people to just give it to you. Institutions have donated money to ventures in the form of grants for years. Today, ventures use donor-based crowdfunding platforms to raise small amounts of cash from many customers and fans in exchange for rewards, such as a discount on the first run of a product or high levels of service. For startups with strong, aspirational branding, consumer products, and/or extremely motivated customers, this can be a great source of cash.

Where does it come from?

- Kickstarter

- Indiegogo

- Crowdfunder

How Funding Rounds Work[*]

Say a couple of scrappy and innovative founders come up with a brilliant new idea. In order to work on this idea, those founders decide to raise a small amount of cash from their friends and family, say, $250,000. In startup-speak, we would say this startup is in the seed stage. This is their first funding round—the first time they take on debt or equity to grow the venture. They use this money to live on and build a prototype.

Then, six months to a year later, those same founders will hit a point where they will need to raise more money, probably to hire more people and build a minimum viable product (the crappiest version of the product a customer is still willing to pay for). This time, they need more cash than their rich uncle can afford, maybe somewhere around $2.5 million. So, they decide to look to the local rich people in their area who invest in startups. These people, called angels, are often successful entrepreneurs themselves and either invest alone or band together with others in the area to form angel groups that help carry the load of finding and filtering startups that are good investments. With this new group of investors, our founders have entered the Series A round of funding.

Since we're making things up, let's say everything goes exactly as planned. Now, the startup has grown into a profitable or soon-to-be-profitable company. The founders decide they need even more money to take the company to scale, say, $10 million. With this amount of money, they can't play around. They decide to go after institutional funding called venture capital (VC). VC firms are startups themselves; a founder raises money from high-net-worth investors like family investment offices, pension funds, and insurance companies and uses that money to invest in startups that will earn the investors a high return. With this funding, the venture has entered the growth stage and raised a Series B.

This process continues, with more and more money being raised from bigger and bigger sources, all the way until the company makes an initial public offering and goes public or is acquired by a bigger corporation.

Let's sum up our mythical company's journey:

Series seed round. Friends and family ($250,000)

Series A round. Angel investors ($2.5 million)

Series B round. Venture capital ($10 million)

That is the story of how funding rounds work. Raise a little money from one group of investors, make progress, and then raise more money from more investors. Paul

*Paul Graham has done an excellent narration of the way startups move through funding rounds; our scenario is inspired by his. See http://www.paulgraham.com/startupfunding.html.

Graham, founder of the accelerator Y Combinator, compares funding rounds to shifting into the right gear. Like a bicycle or car, a venture-backed company moves through several gears, or rounds, of funding as it grows. Each of these rounds gives the venture a boost of cash that allows it to move at an increasingly fast speed. The right kind and amount of funding will move your venture at exactly the right speed, moving the venture fast enough to take advantage of the opportunity before it but not so fast that you lose control and can't make changes as you grow.

Understanding Equity Financing Agreements

Any time a founder sells a stake in his company in exchange for cash, he enters into a legal agreement with whoever gave him that cash. According to Brad Feld and Jason Mendelson in their book *Venture Deals*, that legal agreement is designed to decide two primary things:

1. **Economics.** How the ownership pie gets divided up when the startup is acquired or goes bankrupt (in other words, who gets what, when).

2. **Control.** Who has the power to decide what happens in the business (in other words, who decides what, when).

Investors use a lot of different mechanisms in an agreement to make sure they get the kind of economics and control they want. All the different mechanisms and terms can quickly get confusing. As a founder, your challenge is to decipher the language of investing into what it means for you, your venture, and your stake in it—if the business does very well, if the business does very badly, and everything else in between. We include descriptions of the most important terms here.

Price

Price is the amount investors are paying for an equity stake and what percentage of the venture they get. A correlated term is valuation—the total value of the venture based on the price the investors paid for their shares. Investors look at the issue of price in two different ways.

- **Pre-money valuation.** How much the company is worth before cash is put into it by investors.

- **Post-money valuation.** How much the company is worth after cash is put into it by investors.

This pre-money, post-money thing can get tricky. Pay close attention to which you are talking about during negotiations. You may see other terms related to price on a term sheet; they all come down to the same two things: the amount of cash that is being invested and how much of the company that cash gets the investor. Here are some other ways to present price:

- Price per share

- Percentage of ownership position

- Total invested (aggregate)

Liquidation Preference

Liquidation preference is a way for investors to protect their investment if the venture doesn't do well. They do this by asking for a multiple of their original investment, two times or three times, for instance, when the business is acquired or liquidated. This way, if there isn't enough cash to go around, investors get their money back (and then some) first.

In addition, investors may ask to "participate" as well, meaning that after they've received the multiple of their investment back, they still get their percentage of whatever money is left.

Vesting

Vesting is dividing up the total amount of equity a founder or employee gets over time, so that people who leave the venture early don't get rewarded as much as someone who sticks with it. A typical vesting agreement, or schedule, says that founders or employees will earn their shares over a four-year period, gaining $\frac{1}{48}$ of their shares every month. Usually, there is also a stipulation that they must be with the venture for a full year before they get anything. This one-year rule is referred to as a "one-year cliff."

Not-Quite-Equity Agreements

There is one other thing we should mention about early-stage financing agreements. Often, very-early-stage companies will raise money but want to avoid a valuation—having a price set on how much the venture is worth. They do this because it is too early to decide in any rational way how much the company is worth. In these scenarios, the founders may want to raise money through a convertible note—an equity agreement that starts out as debt and then automatically converts into equity the next time the venture raises money. In exchange, the investor can negotiate a discount on the future shares his money will buy. At the end of the day, the basic goals of the agreement don't change—you are still making decisions about who gets what when and who decides what when—but the terms for convertible notes are different.

9

Overview of Funding Sources

Who invests in startups? Five funding sources make up the vast majority of where startups get money. Each source differs in how much money it invests, at which stages it invests, and in what it brings to the table in addition to funding.

Key Elements:

- Friends and family

- Crowdfunding

- Accelerators

- Angel investors

- Venture capital firms

The Five Funding Sources

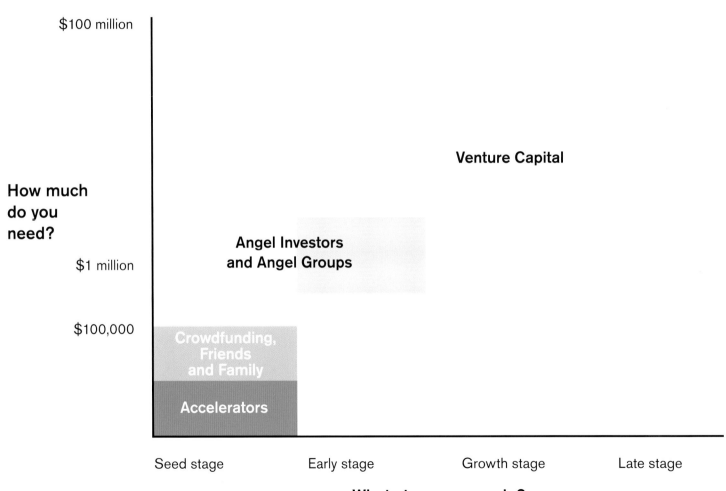

$100 million

How much
do you
need?

$1 million

$100,000

Venture Capital

Angel Investors
and Angel Groups

Crowdfunding,
Friends
and Family

Accelerators

Seed stage   Early stage   Growth stage   Late stage

What stage are you in?

Friends and Family

At a Glance

How much? $5,000–$100,000

When? Seed stage

A scrappy, talented guy decides to go out on his own to launch or buy a business. Without a huge network of seasoned "finance" people, he turns to the most business-minded and/or wealthy people he knows: a rich uncle, the family doctor, the neighbor who found out his ranch sat on a few million dollars of shale oil. That's the typical story of finding "friends and family" investors.

According to one study, 82 percent of all funding for startups in 2012 came from friends and family of the founders. As a group, it is the largest funding target in the United States (and probably the world). In 2011, friends and family invested a total $50 billion, far more in total money invested than venture capital and angel investment combined.

If you plan to take money from friends and family, make sure you are up front and honest about the risks associated with the venture. The reality is, most startups fail, and they need to know they could lose all their money. If losing their investment would significantly hurt the family member's or friend's finances, don't do the deal. As a rule of thumb, you don't want to ask for more than 5 percent of someone's net worth, ideally much less.

Pros	Cons
Compared to other forms, can be very easy to get.	These people are your family and friends. Many relationships have been hurt by deals gone wrong. You should be very aware of the risks to family money.
Capital comes faster.	Typically, they don't provide that much capital.
Leverages the trust you've already built.	Some investors are deterred by messy investor groups, so don't invite too many family members.
Typically, more patient.	Not sophisticated.
Better terms.	May hurt future rounds of capital.

Notable Friends and Family

- The rich relative
- Doctors and lawyers
- The corporate exec at church
- High school friend

Crowdfunding

At a Glance

How much? $5,000–$100,000

When? Seed stage, early stage

Crowdfunding is a very different and potentially disruptive form of startup fundraising that involves many investors pooling small amounts of cash to fund a venture or some aspect of it. Crowdfunding can be divided into two categories:

- **Rewards-based.** People act as "patrons" instead of investors, giving cash in exchange for different levels of rewards. In some cases, those rewards are presales of the product. This is what most people think of when they think of crowdfunding. Examples include the platforms Indiegogo and Kickstarter.

- **Equity-based.** People make actual investments in exchange for equity in a venture. In the past, equity-based crowdfunding platforms could legally accept only accredited (read: rich) investors. With the new SEC rules that came out through the JOBS Act in March 2015, equity-based crowdfunding now extends to almost anyone. Examples include the platforms CircleUp and Crowdfunder.

Crowdfunding platforms can do a lot more than just raise capital. Entrepreneurs use them as marketing tools, to validate a prototype or concept, to collect presales, and to test things like pricing and messaging.

Pros	*Cons*
With rewards-based platforms, you don't have to give up equity.	Everybody sees it. You may not get enough traction on the site, which looks bad if the funding campaign didn't pan out.
Offers you immediate feedback on the viability of your idea; bad ideas don't get funding.	Donors can be impatient and may complain if you don't deliver rewards on time and as promised.
Creates word-of-mouth advertising.	Competitors see what you are doing, which may incite copycats.
Creates a built-in customer base of people who liked your business enough to invest in it.	

Notable Crowdfunding Platforms

- Kickstarter
- Indiegogo
- CircleUp
- Crowdfunder

Accelerators

At a Glance

How much? $5,000–$50,000

When? Seed stage, early stage

They've been called the MBA for entrepreneurs. For early-stage, prefunded companies, these organizations can take your good idea and put it on steroids.

Accelerators are more often runways to funding rather than sources of funding themselves. Admission to one can get you access to capital, idea refinement, developers, co-working space, and validation. Billion-dollar companies have been birthed from accelerators, including Airbnb and Dropbox. Many accelerators also give you access to investors, vendors, suppliers, and potentially other cofounders. Companies typically have to give up a small slice of equity in return for the network the accelerator provides.

Be aware that entrance into an accelerator comes with a particular set of relationships, capital sources, and brand, so choose wisely. As the number of accelerators increases, the quality of the programs and the deals coming out of them will decrease. As a result, more accelerators are specializing in specific verticals.

Pros	Cons
Increase the likelihood of raising money.	Not a great option if you need lots of cash quickly.
Relational capital is very helpful to get intros and feedback on your venture.	The good ones can be extremely selective.
Creates word-of-mouth advertising and PR.	Time consuming and potentially distracting due to all the meetings.
Training and increased business skills.	They can be expensive; many require that you give up a high percentage of equity for a small amount of cash.
Peer advice and support through cohort companies.	Tons of advice can be confusing (five different mentors can have five different pieces of advice).

Notable Accelerators

- Y Combinator
- Techstars
- 500 Startups
- Seedcamp

Angel Investors

At a Glance

How much? $150,000–$500,000

When? Seed stage, early stage

Angel investors are rich people who professionally invest their own money into early-stage companies. Some of the best businesses of the last thirty years started out with investments from angels, including Google, Yahoo, Amazon, Starbucks, Facebook, Costco, and PayPal. An angel's investment tends to be quicker and more personal than investments from venture capital firms. One of the TreeHouse investors put $50,000 in the company without ever meeting Loomis in person because he worked in the home improvement space and liked the concept. The first Outbox meeting yielded a $100,000 investment from a technology angel investor. Many angels are entrepreneurs themselves. There are also angels who are former or current corporate leaders and business professionals.

Pros	Cons
Angels often invest in spaces they have an expertise in and understand.	Some angels may not be well respected. Entrepreneurs should ask the same questions investors ask themselves: Do I like you, do I trust you, do I want to do business with you?
Some angels may even work in the same industry as you. This is categorically "smart money," and other angels love to follow these types of investors.	They get involved, which may not be a good thing.
They can introduce you to lots of other investors, suppliers, and other relationships.	You'll need lots of them to raise enough money, which can be like herding cats.
If they get in on the first round and like what they see, then they may save you the hassle of doing another road show for your second round of financing.	Many angels don't bring anything to the table other than money.

Notable Angel Investors

- Peter Thiel
- Mike Maples
- Dave McClure
- Naval Ravikant

AngelList

Overview

At a basic level, AngelList is the LinkedIn for startups—a directory for finding and researching great startups. Many of the biggest seed venture capital firms and angel investors are on the list, and many use it to help them source and validate deals. But AngelList is also a crowdfunding platform, a way for startups and investors not only to connect with each other but also to actually raise money through what AngelList calls syndicates. Most startups that are on the list and do well raising money with AngelList are in their seed or A round.

AngelList as a Directory for Startups and Investors

Even if you aren't likely to raise money on AngelList, it may be worth creating a profile there for both you and your company. Follow people who you find interesting; do due diligence on your competition. Search for great designers and engineers to hire.

(continued on following page)

Raising Money on AngelList

Posting your profile to AngelList is very easy, but that doesn't mean it is easy to raise money through it. Many founders are tempted to bet on a build-it-and-they-will-come strategy with AngelList: get your profile out there and then sit back and wait for some rich billionaire to reach out wondering how you came up with such a brilliant idea and where he can send the money. This is the lottery scenario. The vast majority of ventures on AngelList raise no money at all. Those that do pay attention to how the round dynamics and momentum affect their strategies. If you plan to try to raise money on AngelList, here's what you should pay attention to:

- **Connect every influential person you can to your profile in any way possible.** You can list people as informal advisers, employees, even as customers, and ask them to give you a testimonial. The more people who are connected to your profile, the more people who will see your profile when you raise money. You want to make your company look as if you have a really great set of friends and supporters.

- **Raise before you raise.** The most ideal time to post on AngelList is *after* you have already raised at least a third, if not half, of the total amount of the money you want to raise. Most investors are likely to rely on the due diligence that other lead investors have

already done. If you already have some major supporters, lots of additional people will be interested in taking part in something someone else has already done the homework on. Also important is the quality of those investors. The more well known they are and the larger their followings on AngelList, the better.

- **Know what kind of money you are trying to raise.** AngelList helps you raise money in two ways. First, it helps provide introductions to larger investors, including traditional VC firms. When these seed firms ask for an introduction or reach out to you on AngelList, they are beginning a conversation that will likely evolve in the same way it normally would outside of AngelList. You probably start with a phone call, maybe followed by a meeting in person. If someone chooses to invest, it will feel just like a traditional round—lawyers putting together documentation, wire transfers, and so on. The other mechanism that AngelList has created for investing is called syndicates. Syndicates are ways for angel investors to pool together much smaller investments, $1,000–$10,000, and co-invest it in a venture. In a syndicate, a group of angels precommit capital that is unlocked every time the syndicate's lead angel invests in a startup. With syndicates, AngelList handles the logistics of the actual financing, including validating that an investor is accredited and handling the transfer of money. AngelList takes 5 percent of each deal done in the platform.

Why You Would Raise Money from a Syndicate

While a traditional seed firm may invest $500,000, a seed investor on AngelList may invest only $5,000. Thus, for your round, you may have dozens of small investors come together to form a pool of $500,000. If your company is the kind that needs lots of support, maybe launching in different geographical markets, getting the word out, or sending you business, AngelList presents a way for you to engage a special kind of fan—the investor fan.

Venture Spotlight: Outbox

For Baehr's first venture, Outbox, he chose to raise money through AngelList. At the time, he closed the second-largest amount ever raised on the platform. Here's his story.

We were interested in raising a Series A and knew we'd likely have one lead institutional investor. We decided to raise money alongside our traditional investor from AngelList for two reasons:

1. We wanted to see if we could raise an additional million or two to increase the overall size of our round beyond what the lead institutional investors had planned to do.

2. We wanted to find a way to engage dozens, maybe even hundreds, of people in our future success as a company. In that sense, AngelList was, for us, a way to connect with different kinds of investors. Given that they are investing significantly less money, there will obviously be significantly more people involved in your round.

We were advised that we should have lined up a major institutional investor and 50 percent of the capital before we posted to AngelList. When we actually posted on AngelList, we published that we had already closed $2.5 million of the total $4 million round. Over the following week, we received introductions and offers for an additional $8 million. In the end, we ended up closing $2.5 million from investors through AngelList. About $2 million of that came from only a handful of people who were actually institutional investors and had their own funds. The other $500,000 came from about forty individuals who were bundled through the AngelList invest online product. This gave Outbox an added fifty people who were rooting for our success and wanted to be helpful however they could.

Anatomy of an AngelList Profile

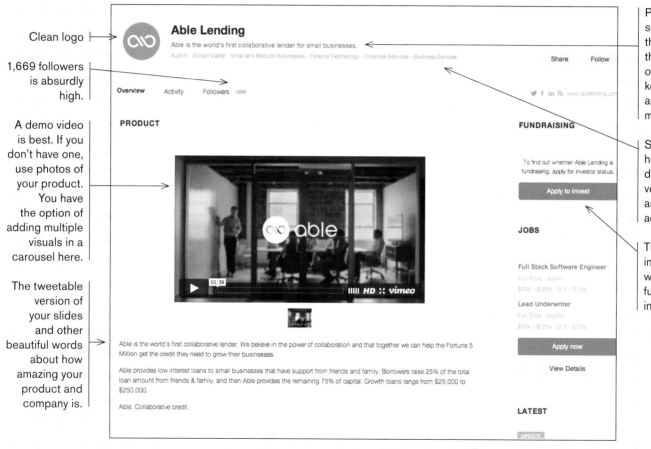

Clean logo

1,669 followers is absurdly high.

A demo video is best. If you don't have one, use photos of your product. You have the option of adding multiple visuals in a carousel here.

The tweetable version of your slides and other beautiful words about how amazing your product and company is.

Able Lending
Able is the world's first collaborative lender for small businesses.
Austin · Silicon Valley · Small and Medium Businesses · Finance Technology · Financial Services · Business Services

Share   Follow

Overview   Activity   Followers 1699

PRODUCT

01:38 |||| HD :: vimeo

Able is the world's first collaborative lender. We believe in the power of collaboration and that together we can help the Fortune 5 Million get the credit they need to grow their businesses.

Able provides low interest loans to small businesses that have support from friends and family. Borrowers raise 25% of the total loan amount from friends & family, and then Able provides the remaining 75% of capital. Growth loans range from $25,000 to $250,000.

Able. Collaborative credit.

FUNDRAISING

To find out whether Able Lending is fundraising, apply for investor status.

Apply to Invest

JOBS

Full Stack Software Engineer
Full Time · Austin
$70k - $125k · 0.1 - 0.5%

Lead Underwriter
Full Time · Austin
$70k - $125k · 0.1 - 0.5%

Apply now

View Details

LATEST

UPDATE

People will see this when they browse through the list of startups, so keep it short and make it memorable.

Search tags help others discover your venture. They are worth adding.

This is where investors would see your fundraising info.

Most bios answer the questions: *Where did you study? Who have you worked with? What do you call yourself?* They are all about social proof—using some institution's credibility that you've been a part of to give you credibility. Other things you can or should add to your profile: your role in the venture; one defining accomplishment; results of work in dollars.

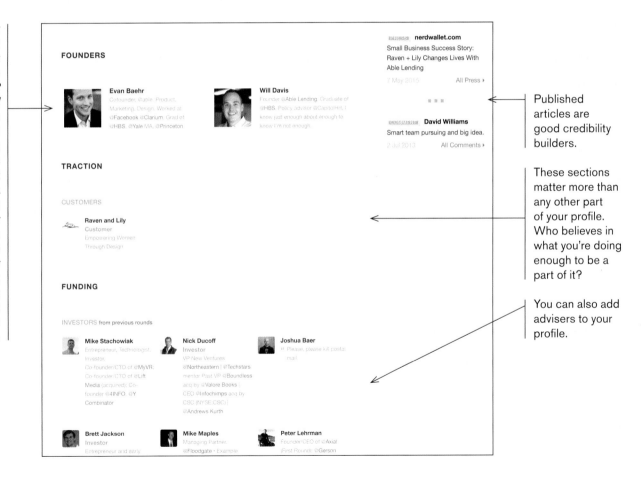

Published articles are good credibility builders.

These sections matter more than any other part of your profile. Who believes in what you're doing enough to be a part of it?

You can also add advisers to your profile.

Venture Capital Firms

At a Glance

How much? $1 million–$300 million

When? Early stage, growth stage, late stage

VC firms are companies that pool money from foundations, insurance companies, pension funds, and institutional investors and invest that money into high-risk ventures for equity.

VC firms are startups. A team of founding partners has a vision for making money by buying equity in other early to midstage ventures. In order to create a fund large enough to pay for those equity stakes, they have to raise money. The founding partners must convince their investors that they have access to amazing startups and entrepreneurs and the ability to recognize great businesses in very early stages. According to the National Venture Capital Association, the average VC fund is $149 million. Because of the high-risk nature of the kinds of investment VC firms make, funds expect a very high return on their investments.

Pros	*Cons*
Social proof. Raising funds from a well-respected VC firm is a powerful signal.	They have the leverage to drive down your valuation.
Lots of cash.	You lose control.
"Smart" money—they often have a depth of experience.	There is an expectation that you will sell the company.
Allows you to scale quickly.	VC firms can put a lot of pressure on their portfolio companies, especially if the fund is near retirement and investors want their money back.

Notable Venture Capital Firms

- Kleiner Perkins Caufield & Byers
- Greylock Partners
- Andreessen Horowitz
- Sequoia Capital

What All Funding Sources Have in Common

No matter which funding sources you pursue, all have one thing in common: they exist to find you.

Without access to deal flow—a steady stream of high-potential ideas and ventures—funding sources die. Some investors like to make entrepreneurs feel as if the power dynamics are heavily weighted to their advantage. They're not.

Broader economic trends ebb and flow. Sometimes, there is more money to go around than there are ventures to put it in. Other times, it's the opposite. At the end of the day, both sides need each other and get the most out of treating each other as respected peers.

Don't get nervous about it, realize you have some of the leverage and power as well because it's the investor's job to meet with you. If you shadowed a VC for a month, you'd see it is their job to have deal flow and to understand what is happening out there and what are the popular deals.

—*Jeff Avallon, Cofounder, IdeaPaint*

Questions You Need to Ask Yourself before You Raise Money

Deciding whether or not to take equity funding is a big decision. These questions help you break down your thinking as you consider raising money and from which funding sources.*

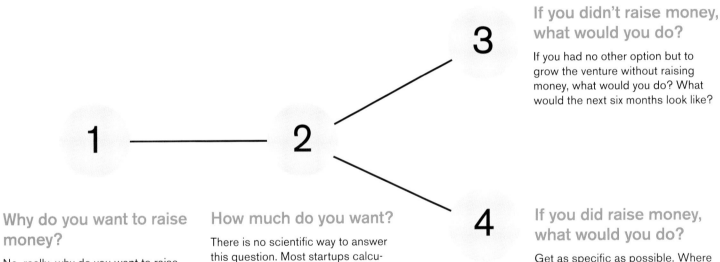

If you didn't raise money, what would you do?

If you had no other option but to grow the venture without raising money, what would you do? What would the next six months look like?

Why do you want to raise money?

No, really, why do you want to raise money? To quit your day job? Hire more people? Reassure yourself it's a good business? Feel cool at a cocktail party? Get all of those reasons out and on paper—the financial, psychological, and business cases for raising a funding round.

How much do you want?

There is no scientific way to answer this question. Most startups calculate the amount they want to raise by starting with a milestone they want to achieve (say, a minimum viable product or cash flow breakeven), and then planning backward to identify the people and resources they will need to get there.

If you did raise money, what would you do?

Get as specific as possible. Where would you spend each dollar? When would you spend it? Who would you hire? What are their names? What resources would you buy or build? This exercise may make you uncomfortable; push through it.

*Thanks to Jeff Avallon, cofounder of IdeaPaint, for suggesting some of these questions.

Introduction to the Friendship Loop

When Francis Pedraza landed in Silicon Valley looking to get his startup, Everest, off the ground, he knew a whopping total of four people there. So, the first thing he did was ask those four people to coffee.

Having just graduated from Cornell, he moved to the West Coast to create an app that helps people live their dreams. He had no team and no resources, just a fire in his belly and a conviction that what he was doing would change the world. A lot rode on those four people.

With each meeting, he focused on building a strong connection with the people he met. He pitched the idea and listened to their feedback. He asked questions and looked for ways that he could add value to their lives by sharing what and who he knew with them. Then, he asked them to introduce him to three people and, without fail, followed up. Within a few weeks, he had every breakfast, lunch, and dinner booked with someone new. These meetings led to introductions to people like Peter Diamandis from the X Prize Foundation and Dave Blakely from IDEO, both of whom agreed to join the board of advisers. The more he engaged with people, the more they wanted to help him. Some entrepreneurs were making ten introductions for him.

Six months later, when he decided he was ready to raise money, Francis had a substantial list of advisers to turn to—a list that would eventually lead to an investment from his childhood hero Bono (more on that later). What made Francis so good at building a network of people willing to help him?

Francis engages in a strict discipline of connecting, cultivating, and following up with people that we call the friendship loop. It's a process focused on relationship building, runs on trust, and takes advantage of often overlooked opportunities to delight others and invite them to be part of the adventure. It's a process used—intuitively or intentionally—by every successful and well-respected entrepreneur we've met. It's also the most ignored aspect of successfully raising money.

Fail to Meet the Right People, Fail to Get the Right Cash

When founders realize that they need to raise money, many react like a man falling backward off a cliff: they find whatever's in front of them and grab like hell. The lure of insta-cash and the fear of the unknown distort the founders' vision so that they begin to treat their relational networks like a series of slot machines to be pulled. Know which machines pay out, discover the right ways to play, and eventually you'll hit the jackpot.

When their immediate networks turn up empty, or if they are too ashamed to ask people they know to invest their own personal savings, the founders start looking for institutional money—venture capitalists, bankers, and established funds. Although a very small percentage of startups meet the criteria for this kind of financing, many founders seek them out because they are much more visible, the process for applying appears straightforward, and there's a certain aura of cool that comes from "going out for VC." Months later, having been strung along by a half dozen responses like "come back to me when you have a lead investor" and hundreds of unanswered e-mails, the founders fold their hands and admit defeat, telling themselves that it just must not have been the right opportunity, never realizing they were toast from the beginning.

The Three Snares

Lost in the moment, founders can often get caught by three seemingly obvious snares during what is known as the road show—the weeks, months, or years an entrepreneur spends raising money.

First, they prioritize cash over relationship. They assume that money is the most important resource their venture needs. It is actually relationships—the vital connections between the right people who have the right resources—that have the greatest impact on a startup's chance for long-term success. Cash burns up faster than you can imagine, but reputation endures. Cash is likely to be the least valuable asset you accrue on a road show.

Second, they assume all money is good money. Entering into a relationship where an investor gives you cash in exchange for ownership in your business is like getting married. That marriage may come with access to new information, industry expertise, or supplier, distributer, or partner relationships. It also may come with burned bridges, control issues, or misaligned incentives, so knowing what investors bring to the table in addition to money should have a significant impact on which people the founders pursue.

Third, some startup entrepreneurs can be terrible stewards of the relationships people offer them. Everyone loves connecting one world-class person to another when it's a gift to both parties. Who wouldn't want to be the guy who introduced someone to his next cofounder or the next entrepreneur who made his $10 million? On the other hand, no one wants to be the guy who introduces someone to the flakey know-it-all who stands people up. Mishandling a well-placed introduction makes everyone look bad. Even though there are a few simple things you can do to leave a lasting positive impression on someone who helps you, few people learn to take advantage of them. There's a better way.

Rather than seeing every high-net-worth individual or firm as a bag of money, entrepreneurs can build relationships with investors whose involvement would be mutually beneficial. They can create such rapport and excitement among the people that they meet that others will go out of their way to help them.

Cash isn't king; friendship is.

We call this paradigm shift the friendship loop, and it starts by taking stock of your personal social graph—who you know and how much access you have to the things and people your startup needs. Starting with the people you already know, you bridge to new social networks by asking for introductions to people they know. Then, you build trust through those new relationships, delight people with gratitude, and invite them to participate in your venture by advising or partnering, introducing you to others who can help you, or investing.

Intro, build, delight, invite. (Repeat). That's the loop.

The Friendship Loop

Intro

to someone who can help move your venture forward.

The first big challenge facing entrepreneurs who are raising money is building trust with the people who have the power to help them. Investors get hundreds of e-mails a day from startups that claim they are launching the next big fill-in-the-blank. What can you do to get them to trust you? You find a bridge. No matter how isolated, every entrepreneur on the planet is one degree from *someone* who can push his or her venture forward. If you can find a bridge to that person through a well-placed introduction, the trust that characterizes the relationship between the person you know and the person you want to know will transfer to you. By starting with the people who are directly in front of you, who already trust you and have an investment in your life, you utilize your own strengths and use your first few warm meetings as opportunities to practice your story, identify unexamined areas of the business, and strengthen your pitching muscle.

Build

a relationship with that person by finding commonalities, asking questions, and "playing" together.

Through that newly transferred trust, successful entrepreneurs get rare opportunities to sit down with potential connectors, advisers, and investors. With pitch decks in tow, they make their ways to coffee shops, restaurants, and home offices. What happens next may be shocking. They shut up and listen. The second step of the friendship loop is to build a relationship. Through finding commonalities that exist between you, through asking questions and listening, and through invitations to play with your idea, killer fundraisers establish genuine connections with the people they pitch to. They seek to understand what each person wants, and they work to help each person accomplish his or her goals.

Delight

through gratitude, follow-up, and thoughtful introductions and resources.

When entrepreneurs follow up with those they meet in sincere and unexpected ways, they turn an ordinary connection into a warm and meaningful memory. Crafting a handwritten thank-you note, sending a thoughtful gift, volunteering time to something the person cares about, and offering valuable connections and resources are the calling cards of friendship loopers. As you'll see later, these small actions can have astonishing consequences when done without expecting anything in return.

Invite

them into the adventure by partnering or advising, introducing you to others, or investing.

The last step of the friendship loop is to extend an invitation to the person you've met. Having carefully thought out what you're asking, how it will benefit both of you, and what needs to happen once that person says yes, you make a clear offer for your new friend to join you on your journey. Whether you are asking him or her to invest in your venture, join your advisory board, or introduce you to new investors, advisers, or experts, you take the responsibility for making it as easy as possible to do whatever it is you are asking.

10

Intro

Man by nature is a social animal.

—*Aristotle*

- Introduction to the social graph

- Build trust with weak ties and super-connectors who can introduce you

- Be aware of your gaps in knowledge and relationships and make them known

- Leapfrog

Before you can talk to investors, you have to be introduced to them.

—*Paul Graham, serial entrepreneur, Founder of Y Combinator*

Reach out to the entrepreneurs who have been funded by the investors you want in on the deal. Make friends with them, pitch them like you would an investor, and when they say "how can I be helpful?" . . . then you say . . . "I have a big favor, can you make an intro for me?"

—*Dan Martell, Founder, Clarity.fm*

We see a lot of startups. The biggest thing that is often underestimated is that the best way to get a VC to get back to you is to get a warm recommendation to them.

—*Tommy Leep, Chief Connector at Rothenburg Ventures, and former Chief Connector at Floodgate Fund*

The people we spoke to first were people who were friends or friends of friends.

—*Adam Tichauer, former President and CEO of Playbutton*

Introduction to the Social Graph

A social graph is a map of your relationships. It provides a picture of connectedness across your professional, personal, and family relationships. They can be massive and amorphous or very simple.

The complexity and shape of your social graph depends on how connected and diverse your network is. By connected, we mean how many people you know. By diversity, we mean how many different kinds of people and groups you know. The more connected and diverse your relationships, the more amorphous your social graph will look. The less connected and more homogenous your relationships are, the simpler it will look. A person with a better connected, more diverse social graph, all other things being equal, will have an easier time raising money. Common sense, right? Well, the significance of your social graph is more subtle—and powerful—than you might think.

Venture Spotlight: Everest

Consider Francis Pedraza. The founder of Everest we introduced at the beginning of this section knew people before he started raising money for Everest. He even knew plenty of different kinds of people. But, he didn't know anyone in Silicon Valley, and he definitely didn't know any investors. He also didn't know many entrepreneurs, designers, or the other key people he needed to make Everest a success.

Like Bono, for instance.

A month before he moved to the Bay Area, if someone had told Francis that the lead singer of U2 would be an investor in his startup, he would have said that person was insane. And yet, six months after launching Everest, there was Francis, sitting at Bono's house in Ireland, listening to him talk about how much he loved the app.

How did it happen? It began with Francis analyzing his social graph.

The Social Graph

The journey from Francis to Bono

5 Fred and Avie decided to invest as individual investors and invited Bono to join them. And, the next thing he knows, Francis is tromping across Ireland with one of the greatest musicians of all time.

1 Knowing that he needed new connections to get Everest off the ground, Francis decided to map his social graph. This is more or less what it looked like—some variations here and there, but, for the most part, everyone he knew knew each other. Much like most people.

2 In order to grow his social graph, Francis tasked John, his intern, with the job of identifying people in Francis's network who knew people Francis wanted to know.

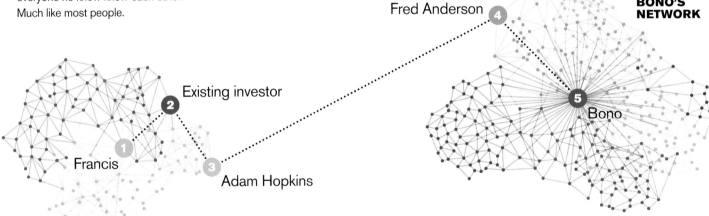

Fred Anderson

BONO'S NETWORK

Existing investor

Francis

Adam Hopkins

Bono

FRANCIS'S NETWORK

3 The intern made a discovery about one of Francis's existing investors. That investor was a friend of Adam Hopkins, a partner at Elevation. Elevation is a private equity firm with investments in Facebook, Forbes, and Yelp, and, coincidentally, was cofounded by Bono.

4 Francis reached out to this existing investor and asked for an introduction to Adam. The investor made the introduction, and Francis pitched Everest to Adam. Adam liked what he heard. He invited Francis to come pitch Fred Anderson and Avie Tevanian, the managing directors of the firm.

Your social graph matters because it helps you identify where and how to start the first step in the friendship loop: bridging from someone you know to someone you want to know. In the same way that a neurologist uses an MRI to identify key issues and prescribe treatments, you can learn to identify and diagnose the character of your social graph in order to discover who you need to be meeting with.

In his book *Where Good Ideas Come From*, Steven Johnson demonstrates that connectedness between normally isolated people and ideas is the primary engine of innovation across history. The relationships you choose to develop decide which ideas and opportunities present themselves to you. If you spend time with only the same people, who spend time only with you, chances are you are going to know the same things, talk about the same things, and like the same things. But if instead you make friends with people who aren't in your group, you get access to all kinds of new information, resources, and opinions. Ronald S. Burt, the sociologist who pioneered this idea, says it this way: "Resources flow disproportionately to people who provide indirect connections between otherwise disconnected groups." Francis says it a bit more plainly: "You have to increase your luck surface area."

Take a look back at the social graph on the previous page. Each of those tiny dots and lines represents a person's communal identity. Imagine what each of those dots represents—the passions, resources, and knowledge within each person. Now, look at just one dot, one in the corner with only two lines extending from it. We'll call her Stacy. On the surface, it would seem that Stacy is a loner, maybe a good gal, but not worth investing in from a fundraising perspective. But remember, Stacy is a social creature just like you; she probably knows as many people as you do, only you don't know any of them. And at least two or three of those people may happen to have a truckload of money.

The distance between you and Stacy's rich friends is what sociologists call a structural hole, and Stacy bridges it. Unlike most of your relationships, the information, connections, and money that Stacy has access to through her rich friends are completely novel to you. You can't get it from anyone else.

What does this all mean? It means you are all literally one introduction away from dramatically altering your social identity and the people, resources, and information you have access to.

That is why intro is the first step in the friendship loop. To build connections with the people who have the power to help your venture, you have to get introductions to them by bridging from someone you know to someone you don't know. You do that by making your needs clear to those around you, building trust with the people you know, and leapfrogging.

Social Graphs 101

STRUCTURAL HOLES

What they are: The spaces between two or more isolated clusters.

What they mean: Find structural holes and be mindful to fill them with new friendships. For example, if you are starting a home improvement company, then you ought to fill in your holes with builders, architects, and designers.

WEAK TIES

What they are: The people on the periphery of your social graph. Most people refer to them as "acquaintances." Weak ties are the highways by which novel resources and information pass between clusters.

What they mean: The most important people in your graph are those you know the least since they have access to people and information you don't.

CLUSTERS

What they are: Each social graph is divided into smaller sub-networks known as clusters. People in the same cluster know a lot of the same people and will have access to the same information and resources. Most people have a work cluster, a family cluster, a school cluster, and a few "club" clusters (church, professional organizations, hobbies).

What they mean: Investors, like all people, run in herds. If you don't have any investors in your clusters, you need to begin to make friends outside of those clusters.

SUPER CONNECTORS

What they are: People who fill many structural holes. Super connectors know a lot of different people from a lot of different clusters.

What they mean: A few people will probably be responsible for introducing you to almost all of the people you need to know. Identifying and enabling these people is one of the most powerful things you can do.

Increasing Your Luck Surface Area

Tommy Leep wants to meet you.

He lives in three different places in the Bay Area, works in Palo Alto and San Francisco, and spends time in public places as much as humanly possible. His job is to run into people. He and Floodgate, the $149 million fund he used to work for, are betting on that kind of connectivity to find the startups that other people don't see and to help the startups they fund succeed:

> My observation from growing up here, and from the research that people have done on Silicon Valley, is that there is a whole ecosystem in Silicon Valley that includes entrepreneurs, investors, banks, lawyers, accountants, PR, journalists, they make the whole ecosystem work, it wouldn't work without the whole ecosystem. So, it's important to know as many people as possible in that ecosystem and help them get what they want. That way, should an awesome entrepreneur come along, we are in a position to help them by connecting them to people in other parts of the ecosystem.

The bet is paying off: Chegg and Twitter, both Floodgate companies, IPO'd in 2013.

With the Tommys of the world out roaming subways and cafés looking for people to bump into, the chances of an unexpected encounter that could lead to something bigger increase significantly. The most important interaction of your road show will very likely be unplanned, unrehearsed, and accidental.

How to Increase Your Luck Surface Area

1. **Make your needs known.** Nobody can help you unless he or she knows how to.

2. **Talk to everyone.** Even the strange guy next to you in the airport terminal. The world is a lot smaller than you think.

3. **Work in public spaces.** Subways, airports, coffee shops. Every town has at least a few restaurants and coffee shops where deals tend to get done. The easiest way to get a chance encounter with a well-known angel or VC is to frequent the places they frequent.

Be Aware of Your Gaps in Knowledge and Relationships and Make Them Known

When Evan Baehr and his cofounder Will Davis started raising money for their first startup, Outbox, they made two lists. The first was a list of one hundred people they knew or had a connection to who they thought could write a check for $50,000. The second was a list of things they knew nothing about but would have to become experts in to make Outbox a reality. The core concept of Outbox was Dropbox for your snail mail, so their list was filled with items like:

1. Knowledge about the US Postal Service.

2. Building labor forces.

3. Hiring developers in Austin, Texas.

4. Big media and ad agencies in New York City.

5. Partnerships with consumer internet companies in Silicon Valley.

Eventually, they came up with about twenty criteria that they used to evaluate possible investors. The more they focused on their needs as a business, the more they began to see financial capital as a commodity. Sure, they needed to get enough commitments to reach $1.5 million (the rough estimate they figured they would need to support the team for eighteen months). But more than money, they needed smart people who were willing to help out with the business.

Let your needs for things other than cash guide your strategy to building new relationships and then make those needs known to those around you. People will know much better how to help you when you tell them what you need. The more concrete your needs, the better. Far from making you look stupid, leading with your needs shows the people you meet that you have a clear grasp of what it takes to make your venture a reality. You'll also save yourself from well-meaning introductions that don't lead to anything and increase your chances of making a connection that is mutually beneficial.

Your Two Lists

Take ten minutes now and start the hard work of making your version of the two lists. Make it a goal to write down ten names and ten needs before you move on. We've given you some sample categories to get you thinking.

Our People List

1. *Rich aunt*

2. *Small business owner at church*

3. *Local Chamber of Commerce*

4.

5.

6.

7.

8.

9.

10.

Our Needs List

1. *Industry expertise*

2. *Renting office spaces*

3. *E-mail marketing tactics*

4.

5.

6.

7.

8.

9.

10.

Build Trust with Weak Ties and Super-Connectors Who Can Introduce You

Introductions have the power to change how a person you meet thinks of you. With a great introduction, you get to share in the trust that your connector has built with the person he or she is connecting you with. Trust transfers.

The transfer of trust is what kept us from getting beat up in middle school the first time a new friend invited us to sit down at the popular kid's table.

> "What's this guy doing here?"

> "He's cool. He's with me."

> "Alright, cool. Let's go dump trash in the choir room."

Statistically, weak ties and super-connectors will be the most valuable resources in your network. In the next chapter, we will go into more depth on how to build a connection with those you meet, but you can start by looking for ways to add value to the lives of weak ties and connectors you know. For instance, pay attention to resources that might be valuable to them—an article or an event related to their industry or people in your network that they would want to know. You can also reach out and ask them for help. Appeal to the person's expertise. Let her know why her input and feedback are so valuable to you.

In order for an introduction to be successful, there has to be some level of trust built up between you and the person introducing you. Before you ask for an introduction, ask yourself:

- What is the level of trust between this person and me?

- What is the level of trust between him or her and the person I want to be introduced to?

- What motivation does this person have for introducing me?

- What motivation is the investor likely to think he has?

E-mail Script: Building Trust through Asking for Feedback

Scenario: Reaching Out to a Close Relationship for Feedback

Subject: Lunch for your feedback?

Begin with something personal and congratulatory. → Hi Jim, I heard that you ran a marathon recently. Congratulations! What a huge accomplishment.

Quick question for you:

Be specific about why you are reaching out and why his or her feedback will be valuable. → I'm launching a new venture called TreeHouse and I'd love to get your take on the concept, especially given your love for sustainability.

Can I take you to lunch in the next couple of weeks? My treat.

I'm available:

Give three different options to minimize the back-and-forth of scheduling. → • Monday, August 1, anytime 11 a.m.–2 p.m.

• Tuesday, August 2, at noon

• Friday, August 5, anytime, 11 a.m.–2 p.m.

But I'll work around your schedule. How does Congress Café sound?

Best,
Evan

Leapfrog

Leapfrogging is the practice of asking others about people they know who might be helpful to you.

Pick five people you know who might be able to help you with your goal and ask if you can bring them coffee and have a short conversation. At the end of your meeting, ask, "What two people come to mind who might be helpful here?" Asking for three people is greedy. One is lame. Just ask for two. Give them a minute to think about it and wait for them to name two people. Mention that you'd love an introduction and that you will follow up.

E-mail Script: Forwardable Intro

Subject: Thanks! // Intro to Jason?

Dear Jim,

Acknowledge that you know how valuable their time is and show that you are aware and applaud them for their success in what they are doing. → Thank you so much for your time and wisdom today. I know you are slammed with the success you've had with Loop, so I'm especially grateful. Since we met, I've been thinking about what you said about the importance of gratitude; it is a really great way to frame how we are thinking about our business. ← Mention something they said or contributed.

Thank you also for the offers to connect me with Jason. I'll follow up with a separate e-mail that you can reference to make an introduction really easy for you.

Sincerely,
Evan

Subject: Intro for AcmeCorp?

Dear Jim,

Give the three-second hook/elevator pitch. → Thank you so much for meeting with me to discuss our new venture: AcmeCorp, the first brick-making company that doesn't suck.

Mention the reason they recommended the introduction. → Thanks for offering to introduce me to Jason. As you mentioned, it sounds like he'd have a lot of insight about how to navigate manufacturing issues. I'd love to connect with him.

Sincerely,
Evan

PS: As background for Jason, I've included a blurb below on AcmeCorp and my background.

About [Company Name]: [150 word description of your company]

About me: [50 words about you]

E-mail Script: Copy/Paste Intro

Subject: Thanks! // Intro to Jason?

Hi Jim,

Thank you so much for meeting with me this morning. I really appreciate getting your feedback about the EdTech case, product direction, and fundraising decks. I would appreciate getting your feedback on my deck as I get it ready for my NYC road show.

> Cast a vision for a continued relationship, without putting the onus on the other person.

Also, would you please introduce me to Jason at Arden? An e-mail you can copy and paste is below. After our meeting, I talked to my product guys and I am confident that we set a schedule to surpass Nisco's expectations. For right now, please hold off on an introduction to Derick.

> Respectfully decline an introduction you're not ready for.

Again, thanks and good luck with the new house!

—Evan

> Add a specific and personal note to help build relationship.

––––––––––

Jason,

I hope you're well.

> Elevator pitch a version of "We help —––—— do —––—— by —––——."

I want to introduce you to Evan, the CEO of Form. His company builds personal financial management apps for employer-based financial wellness programs. He is traveling to New York in late April and was hoping to connect with you.

With that, I'll let Evan take it from here.

Best,
Jim

How to Be a Great Introducee

For the person making it, an introduction is a dangerous thing. If the introducee misses the meeting, doesn't do his or her homework, acts rudely, or makes vague or unreasonable requests, it can damage the introducer's relationships and reputation. Many people argue that in a knowledge economy, your network is your single greatest asset—an asset that must be nourished and protected, if need be. Here are some ways to make sure you don't take the introduction for granted.

Follow up that day. Ideally, within the first few hours of the meeting. This keeps you on top of mind and takes advantage of the momentum you've built connecting.

Keep it super-short. Six sentences or fewer. Most busy people get somewhere in the area of a hundred e-mails a day. Even if they spend an hour a day just working on that day's e-mails, that gives them thirty-six seconds to read, process, and respond to each request. Thirty-six seconds. If it takes more than fifteen seconds just to understand what you're asking, you don't leave much time for them to do something about it. (As a reference, it took you about fifteen seconds to read this paragraph.)

Make your contact do as little work as possible. The only thing the person who has agreed to introduce you should have to do is hit the forward button. One way to do this is to e-mail him a general thank-you e-mail and then separate e-mails for each introduction you need. So, if he offers to introduce you to two people, you'll send him a total of three e-mails. In your introduction e-mail, thank him for agreeing to introduce you, express why the connection will be valuable, and include a short paragraph about your venture.

When reaching out or following up with new connections, be very specific about what you are asking for. Never use phrases like, "Can I pick your brain?" or "I'm hoping to network with . . ." Explicitly state your need and what you would like him to do. In the e-mail, you can also suggest a few specific times to meet and tell him you will work around his schedule. Put all times in the time zone of the person you'll be meeting and, if meeting in person, offer to meet at his office or at a place nearby.

11

Build

The purpose of the pitch is to offer something so compelling that it begins a conversation, brings the other person in as a participant, and eventually arrives at an outcome that appeals to both of you.

—Daniel Pink, author, To Sell Is Human

- Three questions all investors ask themselves

- Do your homework

- Plan your opening

- Find commonalities

- Ask great questions and listen

- Play together

You are screwed if you can't make friends with an investor. It signals that you probably can't build a team or recruit key partners, etc.

—*Dan Martell, Founder, Clarity.fm*

I don't put money on anybody I don't like.

—*Mike Rothenberg, Managing Partner, Rothenberg Ventures*

We had the approach from the second I joined, to sit back and talk to as many smart people as possible. We were fully aware that eventually those conversations would turn into fundraising conversations.

—*Jeff Avallon, Cofounder, IdeaPaint*

I'll let the entrepreneur give their whole pitch, and then it turns into a conversation. The conversation is the best part.

—*Tommy Leep, Chief Connector at Rothenburg Ventures, and former Chief Connector at Floodgate Fund*

The private wealth division of a very well-known investment bank has an axiom it discusses with every new employee during training. Potential investors will ask themselves three simple questions during a meeting:

1. Do I like you?

2. Do I trust you?

3. Do I want to do business with you?

And they ask them in that order. Unless someone likes you, they will never stick around long enough to find out if they trust you. If they don't trust you, they will never want to do business with you, no matter how good your deal is. In the end, it's not your pitch deck that decides whether or not you succeed on the road show; it's your ability to answer these three little questions. In this chapter, we walk you through how to build relationships with your new contacts in a way that helps them answer those three questions sooner, rather than later.

In the very early days of the TreeHouse road show, Loomis got an intro through a mutual friend to a billionaire in New York City. "Why don't we meet at my house?" the billionaire suggested. On the day of the meeting, Loomis made his way down Park Avenue, passing by buildings that have housed people like Jacqueline Kennedy Onassis, John D. Rockefeller, and the heir to the Johnson & Johnson fortune. Intimidated, he rang the doorbell. Someone escorted him to the office, which looked more like the library at Harvard. Gorgeous paintings lined the walls. As they sat down, Loomis tried to make small talk.

"I like the artwork," Loomis said. "Was it painted nearby?"

"No," the investor said. "They're Rembrandts." Of course they are.

Feeling insecure, Loomis reached for his pitch deck and started talking about this amazing business idea called TreeHouse. After five minutes of the "show," Loomis could tell the investor was losing interest. What was it? He made a bold move.

"Would it be okay if we stopped talking about TreeHouse? I'm interested in getting to know you better."

"Good," he said. "I was about to ask you to leave my house."

Perspective Taking, First Impressions, and How to Close an Investor in Three Minutes

There are certain clues—eye contact, tone of voice, body language—that give us insight into what a person is thinking. If we can learn to pay attention to those clues, we can start to understand the world from that person's viewpoint. If we can understand the world from his viewpoint, we can anticipate his behavior. We can know what he is going to do (like whether or not he wants to invest in the deal) before he does it.

In the very first moments of interacting with someone, your brain moves through a series of conclusions, some conscious, some not. With a skill that psychologists call perspective taking, you can learn to recognize and even anticipate these initial reactions. Perspective taking is a way of understanding someone's world through his eyes that allows you to anticipate what he might do or say. Peo-

ple often confuse it with empathy, but the two are distinct experiences. Empathy is about emotionally connecting with someone else or *feeling what he feels*. Perspective taking is about understanding someone's thinking or *seeing what he sees*.

Perspective taking is about asking questions like:

- What might this person be thinking and feeling before she enters the room?

- What is she doing and saying when she is in the room?

- And, most importantly, why?

The First Three Minutes

Psychologists have found that humans begin to categorize the people around them within 150 milliseconds of meeting them and, by the end of a first meeting, have likely made character judgments that can endure for a very long time.* In the very first moments of your interaction, here are some of the questions a person may be asking.

*Kimberly D. Elsbach, "How to Pitch a Brilliant Idea," *Harvard Business Review*, September 2003, https://hbr.org/2003/09/how-to-pitch-a-brilliant-idea.

Fifteen Milliseconds: Should I Trust You?

Long before you've said a word, the person you are meeting has made an unconscious mental judgment of you, and you have made one of him. The amygdala—the part of your brain that you share with reptiles and that tells you whether or not to punch someone, run away, or play dead—makes a nearly automatic conclusion about your surroundings. Do I trust this person? Does this person look like someone I might like?

Ten Seconds: What Kind of Person Are You? Are We Connecting?

In the seconds that follow, two other processes begin. The first, referred to by one study as "prototype matching," searches through the listener's preconceived notions and stereotypes to compare and contrast you with what she already knows. Are you the creative type? Can you tell a good story? Can you get the job done? Do you have what it takes? The second process is self-reflective; it pays attention to what the listener is doing and feeling in order to find clues as to the kind of relationship that's being formed. Am I being "swept along" in the magic of something bigger, or am I bored and distracted?

Three Minutes: What Am I Going to Do?

Eventually (in around three minutes), the prefrontal cortex kicks in to start making decisions about what to do with the information the person is taking in. It starts by coming up with a set of potential actions—invest or not invest, for instance—and then doing a risk/reward calculation for each of those actions. Before long, you have a pretty strong idea of which action is worth pursuing.

Exercises to Improve Your Perspective Taking

Read more literary fiction. A recent study found that reading literary fiction can increase a person's ability to recognize someone else's mental state. These kinds of works, according to the research, cause people to use their imaginations to make inferences about what someone might be thinking.

Take an improv class. Improvisers have to pay attention to subtle clues in their partner's words, movements, and body language to fill in the gap of knowledge between them. In other words, they have to learn to read each other's minds.

Lead with the most controversial part of your venture. Choose the most controversial aspect of your pitch, and the next time you meet with someone, make it the first thing you talk about. Then, watch his or her response. Use it as a litmus test for gauging his or her interest in your venture.

Do Your Homework

Want to make sure the person you meet with never answers your e-mail again? Show up unprepared.

Entrepreneurs and high-net-worth people are extremely busy. They have to say no to people every day. They don't do it because they're sadistic (not most of them, anyway); they do it because, if they don't, their lives will literally fall apart. In the time it takes both of you to sit down and sip a latte, most investors will have fifty new demands for their time waiting in their in-boxes. Every minute there is a trade-off between things that are both important and urgent.

Busy people have websites with bios for a reason. Read them. People are flattered when you take the time to find out about them—their interests, prior investments, and especially, mutual relationships. Google is the best place to start. Then, search their LinkedIn profiles, company websites, and board memberships. Pay particular attention to the types of organizations they are involved in. You can find out a lot about a person with five minutes of internet research. After half an hour, you should have a solid idea of how you think this person can help you.

How to Research People You Are Meeting

1. **Google their name and review the first two pages of results.** Then, Google their name again, but this time add "filetype:pdf" to the query. It will display only PDF files and will likely turn up work they've written.

2. **Follow them on AngelList.** See what investments they've made recently and who they are connected to.

3. **Follow them on Twitter.** See who they follow and who they're tagging and talking to.*

4. **Use Newsle.** Newsle is a service that syncs with your e-mail, LinkedIn, and Facebook to find news articles on people you're connected to. You can also use it to follow people you want to connect with.

5. **Read their blog.**

What You Should Know about the People You Are Meeting

1. Professional background

2. Mutual relationships

3. Personal interests

4. Boards they serve on, nonprofits they volunteer for or support

5. Marital and family status

*Thanks to Mark Suster and his blog, Bothsides of the Table, for this tip, http://www.bothsidesofthetable.com/2009/06/19/getting-access-to-the-old-boys-club-how-to-approach-a-vc/.

6. Previous deals they've done, companies they've started, and industries and areas they favor

Background Profile Template

First and Last Name

Company/Organization
_____

Profiles

AngelList: _____

Twitter: _____

What They've Written

_____
_____

Mutual Relationships

_____
_____

Deals They've Done

_____
_____

Commonalities

_____
_____

Plan Your Opening

You pull open the glass door to the café and walk through. As you look up, you catch a glimpse of a woman near the counter. She swipes and taps at her phone. You recognize her from the research you've been doing in preparation for the meeting. You approach her, introduce yourself, and offer to buy her a coffee. She accepts, and you both turn to get in line. The noise of grinding espresso and conversation swirls around you. The two of you stand silently, waiting to reach the barista.

What do you say?

By planning out what you say in those first crucial minutes, you will learn how to set the tone of a conversation. Your opening remarks should do six things.

1. Show That It's Not All about Money

There is a palpable awkwardness in any interaction where asking for money is involved. _They_ know you are only meeting to ask for something from them. _You_ know they know you are only meeting to ask for something from them. Inwardly, you are both squirming. But what do you can do about it?

You make it go away by ensuring that your first conversation is *not about money*. Because the reality is, it's *not* all about money, especially at first. In the beginning, your goal, and the goal of the person you are meeting, is to answer the question: "Do we like each other?"

2. Complete the Transfer of Trust

Pay attention to the transfer of trust the next time you sit down with someone you've been introduced to. The conversation almost always goes like this:

> "Hey, Bob, it's great to meet you!"
>
> "Good to meet you as well."
>
> "I'm so glad John put us in touch; he's a great guy. How did you first meet?"
>
> "He saved my dog from a burning building."
>
> "Man, that's just like John."
>
> "It sure is."

Do you see what happened? By connecting over your shared appreciation for your friend John, you completed the transfer of trust that John started when he introduced you and Bob over e-mail.

3. Show Confidence

Stand up straight, look the investor in the eye, and firmly shake his or her hand. Show that you are trustworthy.

4. Put Them at Ease

Everyone is insecure. Even the investors you meet. Of course you're nervous; you're about to put your baby on display and ask for a bunch of money. Recognize, though, that investors get nervous, too. You are a gamble to them. Use the personal information you learned from doing your homework to show respect for them and show that you care and are excited to get to know them better.

5. Make It about Them

Dos Equis has a series of commercials about the "most interesting man in the world." The narrator tells of the feats of actor Jonathan Goldsmith ("He gave his father 'the talk,'" "When he drives a car off the lot, its price increases in value.") The campaign's popularity drives home an important lesson about human nature: everyone has a desire to be perceived as smart and interesting.

When people feel smart, they feel empowered. When they feel empowered, they open up and share their ideas. Sharing ideas is called "play." (More on that soon.)

6. Show Gratitude

Anyone who has enough experience to help you is going to be busy—very busy. That means that they have likely sacrificed something very important to take thirty minutes out of their day to meet with you—a couple dozen e-mails, a lunch with their spouse or an old friend, their midday workout. You recognize that sacrifice by expressing your gratitude.

Scripts for Your Opening

At a Presentation

"I'm so grateful to get to be here today. Thanks for taking the time to share your vision and hear a bit more about what we're up to."

"I'm really grateful to _____ for introducing us. Before I get started, I'd love to hear more about how you first connected with him/her."

At a One-on-One Meeting

"I was really excited when we got connected because . . ."

"So, tell me more about _____. I saw it in your bio, and it fascinated me."

"You and I have something in common . . ."

"I'm really grateful to _____ for introducing us. How did you first get connected with him/her?"

Find Commonalities

Commonalities are the passions and details of life that you share with the people you meet. The mutual friend who introduced you is the most obvious commonality you'll share with the people you meet, but it won't be the only one. Maybe you went to the same alma mater. Maybe you both like hockey, or are coffee aficionados, or are passionate about the same causes. As you research someone's background, search for things that you have in common that you both would enjoy connecting over. Then, bring it up during your meeting.

"You and I are from the same town," you'll say.

"No way," he or she replies.

"What street did you live on?"

"Broadmoor."

"You're kidding me! My cousins live on Broadmoor—the Smiths."

"The Smiths used to babysit me!"

"Small world!"

By this point, you're practically family.

Commonalities to Build Off

- Your mutual friend

- Hobbies

- Causes

- Foreign languages

- Locations—hometowns, favorite places to visit, college towns

Ask Great Questions and Listen

It's easy to get caught up in "nailing the pitch." Especially during those first meetings, your nerves can give you tunnel vision. Overwhelmed by the pressure and the task in front of you, you lose sight of the fact that the person in front of you isn't a cash dispenser and he or she didn't show up to listen to a lecture.

People take meetings expecting to have conversations. So make it a conversation. Get phenomenally interested in the person across from you. His life should be so amazing to you that you would want to write a book about it. If not, why are you meeting with him? Ask questions about his life and listen to his responses. Ask his feedback about specific aspects of the venture. Tell him why you wanted to meet with him and why you think his support would be invaluable to you.

Would you rather give money to the entrepreneur who is sure that he's right and isn't interested in your thoughts? Or to the entrepreneur who is constantly learning and asks for feedback?

One of the most exciting parts of the road show is getting input from your investors. Many of their ideas are worth their weight in gold. At TreeHouse, Loomis made major changes in his business model after speaking with the founders and executives of Home Depot, The Container Store, Neiman Marcus, Ace Hardware, Apple Store, and Whole Foods. If you have the curiosity and humility to ask for feedback, you'll be amazed at what you learn. Make it a point to not argue with what they tell you or try to defend yourself or your idea, even if what you hear sounds insane. Listen, take notes, and say thank you.

Remember, someone you know put trust on the line in order for you to get this meeting. Are you living up to that trust?

Questions You Can Ask

"Can you tell me about the first company you ever invested in?"

"What gets you really excited about a company?"

"What's something you see in early-stage startups that most people don't?"

"What do you believe is true that most people would disagree with you about?"

"What do you think we might not be seeing right now?"

Play Together

Play might sound like an odd description for a first-time meeting with a billionaire angel investor, but that is exactly what most investors do when they are interested in an opportunity. Play implicates them in the venture; it puts them into the driver's seat and causes them to look at the venture from the perspective of someone already involved. What does it mean to "play"?

Jesse Schell, designer of play experiences like Disney's "Toy Story Midway Mania" and "Pirates of the Caribbean," and author of *The Art of Game Design*, says this about play:

I can't help but notice that most play activities seem to be attempts to answer questions like: "What happens when I turn this knob?" "Can we beat this team?" "What can I make with this clay?" . . . When you seek to

answer questions freely, of your own volition, and not because you are obligated to, we say you are curious. But curiosity doesn't immediately imply you are going to play. No, play involves something else—play involves willful action, usually a willful action of touching or changing something—manipulating something, you might say. So, one possible definition would be: Play is manipulation that indulges curiosity.

A key aspect of building a relationship with investors is indulging their curiosity and inviting them into a kind of play that involves your idea. You allow them to make suggestions about how to improve your business model, ask questions about your assumptions, and make connections about how and why what you're doing is going to be world changing.

Make no mistake; letting others play with your idea can be hard. Entrepreneurs have invested a lot of time and heart in their ventures, and opening that venture to whatever brilliant idea the person you talk to comes up with is scary. And yet, this kind of openness is how powerful connections are formed, and it's one of the quickest ways to refine the idea.

Does your venture have a physical component? Bring it. Is there a demo of it? Show it. Can the people you meet with go to something that you've built or created? Bring them there. Then, get out of the way. Let them play with what you've created and see if they're interested in playing more. If they are, you will get the opportunity to play together.

You can recognize that someone is playing with you when they ask questions like, "What if you changed . . .?" or "Have you thought about . . .?" or when they make statements like, "That could be really great for . . ." These comments are the classic "yes, and . . ." principle of improv in action. They are taking your idea and running with it so that it becomes *our* idea.

When you've done that, you're ready to move on to the next step of the friendship loop.

Venture Spotlight: Karma

"We're building the first mobile provider that doesn't suck." That's the opening line for Steven van Wel and the guys at Karma—a pay-as-you-go mobile Wi-Fi hot spot. They had built a lot of momentum after an accidental encounter with the managing director of Techstars New York and decided to go out for a $1 million seed round. Early on, they realized that there were two things about the nature of their company that either drew people in or repelled them. First, they were hardware. People have an immediate reaction to seeing a physical product—you either like it or you don't. Second, they were a mobile provider. There aren't a lot of successful small mobile providers, and to go after the AT&Ts was going to be a challenge—one you're either up for or you're not.

So, when Steven opened a conversation with a potential investor, he made those two things clear within the first three minutes. "I [would] always bring the hot spot," he said. "The first thing I would do is pull out the device, put it on the table, and just leave it there. I noticed that if people play with it, they like it; if people don't play with it, they don't like it."

In the span of about a month, Steven met with two hundred potential investors. "One hundred eighty people thought we were idiots," he said, "and twenty people really liked us." Many of those twenty people knew they were going to invest within the first three minutes. Steven reflected on it afterward, "That was sometimes really helpful, because if people are excited, they are really excited. It was a helpful way to filter out conversations that would lead to investments."

The guys at Karma used the most controversial aspects of their business as a litmus test for revealing an investor's interest. Instead of focusing on cajoling those who weren't very interested in the first place, they led with what they knew would either scare people off or excite them enough to join. Every great idea has something about it that people will find either brilliant or idiotic. Find out what will create an immediate reaction in potential investors and communicate it as early as possible.

Handling Objections

Every venture has some sore spot it would prefer to gloss over or not mention at all. Often, entrepreneurs won't even see these problem areas until an investor asks about them, and suddenly they find themselves caught with their pants down, wishing they had never taken the meeting.

The easiest way to keep from looking like an idiot in front of an investor is to spend your first meetings getting feedback from people you know and trust. These meetings will help you identify the weak spots in your business and learn how to address them honestly and directly.

You can start to uncover those areas now by asking yourself the following questions:

1. Where are the gaps in our team?

2. What do we lack in experience, knowledge, or relationships?

3. What assumptions do we make in our projections?

4. What are we afraid to ask ourselves?

5. What have we underestimated about our competitors?

6. What are our greatest risks?

7. What's in it for me? Who knows that?

No matter how much you prepare, you will still get questions about your venture that you don't know how to answer. Own your ignorance. A simple, "I don't know the answer to that, I will get back to you" builds trust and gives you an opportunity to follow up. You can also ask investors for their feedback by saying something like, "That's a challenge we're still trying to solve. This is what we are doing right now to solve it, but do you have any feedback?" Don't give a BS answer. It just makes you look stupid.

In your meetings, if investors ask you several of the same questions over and over again, add them in a FAQ slide in the back of your deck.

12

Delight

"Can I do anything for you, Mr. Bond?"
"Just a drink. A martini, shaken, not stirred."

—Goldfinger

- Follow up immediately

- Send a handwritten thank-you note

- Give a thoughtful gift

- Make specific offers of your network and resources

There was this one investor we really wanted to have onboard. They weren't having it. I got an existing investor to write a follow-up e-mail. I spent two hours writing a two-line e-mail to him. The investor who backed me said, "Incidentally, that was a really effective email."

—*Sanjay Dastoor,*
  Cofounder, Boosted Boards

The meeting went fine, but Loomis could tell he wasn't interested. They stood up, and Loomis thanked him for his time. They shook hands and left the café. A few weeks later, Loomis remembered a small detail about the conversation.

During the first few minutes, the investor had mentioned that he and his wife were preparing for an anniversary trip in the Mediterranean. Having known about the area the investor mentioned, Loomis asked what hotel they were staying at. Loomis didn't recognize the name, but he wrote it down in his notes after the meeting. Weeks later, Loomis remembered that their anniversary was in a few days. As a gesture of kindness, he had an assistant contact the hotel to send a bottle of wine to the investor's room with a note. Then he forgot about it. A month later, he got a letter from the investor in the mail with one sentence:

"I'm in for $250,000, thanks for being so thoughtful."

$100 well spent.

Thoughtfulness expressed through acts of gratitude is one of the rarest and most powerful characteristics an entrepreneur can possess. Handwritten letters, a small but personal gift, or just doing what you say you will are so out of the ordinary in today's culture that they surprise and delight people—sometimes so much so that it motivates people to act.

The third step in the friendship loop—delight—is a founder's opportunity to demonstrate their sincere interest in the person they meet with, not just in what they can get from that person. There are an infinite numbers of ways to delight someone. You can show grace or kindness to someone when she is late or forgot something she told you she would do. You can show an extra amount of thoroughness and follow-through in answering a request someone makes of you. You can show a candid amount of honesty and vulnerability about the weaknesses of your venture and how you are planning to tackle them.

All of these examples create the experience of delight in the recipients because they don't expect them. Going beyond someone's expectations is at the core of delight and the guiding principle for founders hoping to delight others. We focus on four key actions that are likely to delight the people you meet with: following up immediately, sending a handwritten thank-you note, giving a thoughtful gift, and making specific offers of your network or resources in ways that benefit others.

Follow Up Immediately

After every meeting, send an e-mail with anything you mentioned or promised during your time together as well as a clear next step for the relationship. Doing what you said you were going to do can be a significant way to delight someone who is used to false promises.

E-mail Script: Following Up

Subject: [Startup Name] Follow-up meeting 12/11

Hi Jason—

Begin with gratitude and something personal. ⊢→ Thanks for your time just now. Your feedback on how to expand our distribution was incredibly helpful.

Add standard boiler-plate pitch. ⊢→ Just for reference, here's a bit about what we are doing—[insert elevator pitch here].

Include pitch deck. ⊢→ I've updated our investor deck; I'd love to get your feedback on this. Here's the link: [link]

I'd love to keep you updated on our progress. I'll follow up every couple of weeks to update you on what we've done.

Thanks,
—Evan
  Cofounder & CEO

Send a Handwritten Thank-You Note

We live in a digital world, but we are analog creatures. Considering the bombardment of electronic messages, the most powerful way you can convey appreciation and intent is through a handwritten note. Far from being outdated, handwritten letters have become even more important as more and more of our lives are digitized.

Types of Material

Correspondence cards. Look like thick postcards with your name at the top. They are usually around four by six inches and work beautifully for follow-ups and thank-you notes.

Fold-over cards. Great for following up also. Fold-overs sometimes provide you with more room to write, so if you have big handwriting, you might consider them.

Letter sheets. Letter sheets should be used for more intimate communication—a letter to a close friend on a special occasion, for instance. Don't use them for new connections or as thank-you cards; you'll run out of things to say way before you've filled up enough of the page.

Letterpress. If you really want to go over the top, you can have your own stationery made by letterpress. It will cost you more, but you'll get that classy, Old World feel of embossed letters.

Brands
- Crane.com
- Americanstationery.com
- Papyrus.com
- Smythson.com
- neimanmarcus.com
- feltapp.com
- hellobond.com

Give a Thoughtful Gift

If you listen closely, you can uncover small details about a person's life and interests that can clue you in to ways to delight him or her with a thoughtful gift. Important events like birthdays and anniversaries, hobbies and interests, and personal causes can all be opportunities to offer something that will be very meaningful. Gifts surprise, disarm, and encourage reciprocity. They help level the playing field between you and the person you are asking something from. What can you send, give, or do for the people you meet with that would wow them? It ought to be personal, something that makes the person feel known and valued.

Ideas for Delighting with Something Unexpected, from Vague to Personal

- Breakfast, lunch, or dinner

- A copy of your favorite book

- Wine

- Cigars

- Gift card to a favorite restaurant

- Tickets to the opera

- Tickets to a sporting event

- Tickets to their favorite band

- Donation in time or money to a cause they support

Make Specific Offers of Your Network or Resources

One of the more surprising discoveries of life during the road show is that you have something to offer to the people you meet. Each time you move through the friendship loop, your social graph expands exponentially. Those new connections give you access to new kinds of information that can be useful to those you meet. So, offer it to them. Pay attention to the goals and needs and find specific resources—news articles, events, or books—that you can send their way.

13

Invite

"Who's coming with me?"

—Jerry Maguire

- How to make an ask
- The different types of asks
- Types of investment asks
- Notes on closing

All right, here's the setup: I'm an angel investor that you're pitching and it's pretty clear that I'm interested and the meeting's about ready to be done. Close me. You just see people try all kinds of random shit. They just don't know how to handle that situation.

—Jason Seats, Managing Director, Techstars, Austin

Some of these people would sit down, and if they liked what I was doing, they would make as many as ten intros for me—very generous. It makes a strong impression when someone goes out of their way to help you.

—Francis Pedraza, Founder of Everest

"It sounds like this is something that you could be really interested in, can we count you in for this round?"

"Would you be willing to come on as one of our advisers?"

"Is this something you would be interested in investing in?"

"Does anyone come to mind who could be helpful here?"

Few people like feeling needy. Asking people for things rubs against our delusion of self-reliance like sandpaper on eyeballs. And nothing gets most founders more uncomfortable than having to ask people directly for money. All of your personal baggage about money will surface the moment you start asking people for it. Suddenly, your parents' nagging words about finances start replaying in your head. All the doubts about the venture that you've been suppressing force their way up. You've been playing entrepreneur long enough; it's time to get a real job. People think you're an idiot. You're wasting your reputation.

What makes "the ask" so awkward for most people? Is it the fear of rejection? Of looking stupid? The fear that—deep down—the venture isn't worth anything and isn't going anywhere? Here's the truth: if you really believe in your venture (and we trust that you do), then the best thing that could ever happen to an investor is the opportunity to invest in your venture.

This isn't false bravado. Every investor knows that the odds are against the startups he or she meets. What investors want—what they spend their careers seeking out—are offers from passionate entrepreneurs who believe they are building ventures that will change the world.

The final step of the friendship loop—invite—is the art of making those offers. This step is rooted in a deep conviction that what you are asking for will make the person's life markedly better. It is literally an invitation, a way to say "I think you're really going to like this" and "let's do something amazing together." To invite others into your venture, you must first decide what your invitation will be. Then, you must break down that invitation into the very next step that the person needs to take. Lastly, and this is going to sound a little silly, you must script your invitation and practice it so that, when your nerves start going haywire, you won't back out or do something bizarre.

How to Make an Ask

Decide What Your Invitation Will Be

Your invitation will depend on which stage of the venture you are in and who you are talking to. Early on, you may want only to keep someone in the loop—an invitation for someone to follow your progress through periodic e-mails or meetings. It's not uncommon to find a cofounder or key partner during this process. You may invite someone to join a formal board of advisers, a group of experts you learn from and consult for wisdom on difficult decisions and problems to help you set the right course for your venture and sometimes serve as a pool for eventual investors. Finally, you can give the big ask: to invite someone to invest a specific amount into your venture.

As you consider your invitation, answer the following questions:

- What do you want from the person?

- What are you offering him or her in return?

- What will you do together?

Break the Invitation Down into the Very Next Step

What happens if the person says yes? As obvious as that question seems, many founders forget to take the time to answer it. Words like "partner," "advise," and "invest" are ambiguous; doing them requires a series of much smaller and concrete actions.

Chip Heath and Dan Heath discuss the principle of clarity in their book, *Switch: How to Change Things When Change Is Hard*. Ambiguous goals, they say, are very difficult to accomplish. By breaking down your invitation into the very next action that you want a person to take, you make it much more likely that he or she will do it. We discuss the process of closing investors in detail in the next section.

Script and Practice Your Invitation

Why does nearly every entrepreneur know that he must practice the first thirty seconds of his pitch but never thinks to practice the last fifteen? Memorize what you plan to say when you come to that moment of truth. As you script the kinds of invitations you make, it's helpful to keep in mind a few things.

Ask Investors a Question

As obvious as it seems, people often fail to make a clear and direct ask. It will feel awkward, but if you don't put people on the spot and ask, "Can we count you in on this round for [x] dollars?" you're in danger of getting a lot of fake yeses. You'll be tempted to leave it at "Well, thanks for listening. Just think about it and let us know . . ." This is a terrible strategy. They will never call you back.

The time to ask is when they are in front of you and your goal is to get them to say out loud, "Yes, I'm in for $x." In many cases, investors won't even know (or ask) about the valuation or deal terms. For many, it simply doesn't matter.

Tell Investors Exactly What You're Looking For

How much money do you need? How many people are you looking to raise money from and at what levels? What do you want from them specifically?

Make Investors the "Missing Link"

People want to feel as if their contribution has a large impact. If you can present what you need in a way that makes their contribution seem like the final piece of a great opportunity, they're much more likely to give.

Surface the Contingencies

The Techstars team teaches their entrepreneurs that if an investor is interested, he is "in," barring some contingency. By directly asking an interested investor what it would take for him to be 100 percent certain he is in, you give him permission to talk explicitly about his hesitations and give yourself the opportunity to address them.

Let Investors Break the Silence

Part of making it easy to say yes is making it difficult to say no. Don't make it easy on them by filling in the silence. Once you've made the ask, do what a friend advised us: pause and take a long, slow sip of water.

The Different Types of Asks

Questions to Ask Yourself

Where am I in my road show? Are you one or two signatures away from finishing the round, or are you hoping to get that first signature? You will need to frame your ask around the phase you are in.

At what level do you want this person to invest? Do you want her to lead the round? How much money can she reasonably invest, based on the types of deals she has done in the past? Decide on a specific number, like $50,000, $250,000, or $1 million.

Is this person really interested? What kind of questions is he asking? Has he been engaged, nodding his head, or has his body language cooled? By the time you ask for money, you should have a good idea of the investor's interest level.

Updates

You will want to invite almost every person you meet to keep updated on your progress through periodical update e-mails. These updates are usually monthly or bimonthly, and they follow a straightforward pattern: what you've done, what you're planning to do, and the needs and questions you're facing right now. Keep these e-mails brief and only include information you would be OK with publishing. We'd recommend creating separate update e-mails for committed investors or advisory board members, where you can include a bit more detail.

Make sure to explicitly ask people before you start sending them updates; don't just add them to some massive e-mail list. At the end of the meeting, ask them, "Would it be OK if I kept you updated on our progress every few weeks?" Most people genuinely will want to know how things are progressing.

Venture Spotlight

Deena Varshavskaya, founder and CEO of Wanelo, shared with us her experience of sending updates to current and potential investors.

What I would do is I would start sending e-mail updates to investors, and I would include the number of monthly uniques in the subject line. When I started fundraising, I was at 100,000 monthly unique visitors. When the first money hit the bank, we were close to a million.

I think sending those updates with nothing but the monthly uniques in the subject line was really helpful . . . Shortly after I got my first investor, Ann Miura-Ko at Floodgate responded to my latest monthly uniques update and said that she was interested in leading the round.

Script for Progress Updates

Thanks to Austin health care startup Filament Labs for letting us use their newsletter for this script:

Only the recipient's name should be visible. Use an e-mail service like MailChimp to send updates or bcc everyone so you don't share others' e-mail addresses.

Subject: Filament Labs Update—Building Momentum

Specific subject line that includes the name of the company. This may be the only thing they read, so don't waste it.

Dear Filament Labs Investors, Advisors, and Friends:

Techstars is now complete, but we're just getting started. ;) You can watch Jason's Demo Day pitch here, and check out the press that resulted.

"Scannable" formatting

Very clear asks ⊢→ **Needs**

Investor intros. Looking for strong angels in health care and SaaS. We love Austin-based investors.

We're hiring! Looking for two strong iOS and Android developers to join our team as #4 & #5, respectively.

Updates

Fundraising is on a roll ($150k+ in new commitments). We're on a road show toward $500k, with $125k already closed, and $150k+ in new commitments since our last investor update e-mail. In addition, Dr. Neiman—a doctor from one of Corinthian's clinics—is interested in joining our seed round in a meaningful way.

Links for people to dig in more if they want to

Filament named to Austin's A-List.

CNN named us one of the Top 5 Austin Startups to Watch.

SXSW and the Austin Chamber of Commerce named us one of the 5 hottest emerging startups in Austin for this year.

UofM invited Jason to tell his story to 400 students.

The University of Michigan invited Jason to tell his entrepreneurial story to 400 students at their ENTR 407 class last week. This is the same class that hosted Jim McKelvey (cofounder, Square), and Tony Fadell (founder, Nest). Check out the video!

Pitch and investor materials

Filament Labs is building a patient engagement platform, giving health professionals tools to manage their patients when they are away from the clinic. We specialize in patient compliance around chronic disease, with an initial focus on the infusion and dialysis space, a 14,000 clinic/$27B market. By early Q1, we will power patient engagement for 20 clinics nationwide. Our first customer is also an investor, with strategic involvement from a large specialty pharmaceutical supplier.

Filament Labs is a Techstars Austin '13 company. Filament's founders have previous exits to WebMD, Expedia, and Rev Worldwide.

Download our investor deck and executive summary, and follow us on AngelList.

Health care fact: Dr. Willem Kolff, a Dutch physician, constructed the first working dialyzer in 1943 during the Nazi occupation of the Netherlands. Due to the scarcity of available resources, Kolff had to improvise and build the initial machine using sausage casings, beverage cans, a washing machine, and various other items that were available at the time.

As always, incredibly grateful for your continued time, interest, and advice,

Jason, Colin, and Brian

Types of Investment Asks

Your ask is a tailor-made request, targeted at the individual you are talking to and based on where you are in the funding process. Consider these five types.

1. Testing the Waters

Scenario: You're not yet ready to raise money. You are concerned about gauging an investor's interest and building the relationship for further down the road.

Script: "We're going to be looking for investors. Is this something you'd be interested in when we're ready to raise capital?"

2. Partnership

Scenario: The potential investor's expertise is just as valuable as his or her money.

Script: "It's clear you have a passion and expertise in this industry. You are exactly the type of partner we will need. Will you consider joining me?"

3. Working with People You Like

Scenario: You sense a strong amount of interest from someone who values impact as much as financial gain.

Script: "Hey, I really like you guys. I think we've got a great opportunity. Why don't we do something amazing together?"

4. Hard Charger

Scenario: You have limited time with a decisive, high-value prospect.

Script: "I've got a big ask for you. Will you invest $1 million?"

5. Momentum

Scenario: You are more than halfway to funding your current round.

Script: "We've already succeeded in finding much of the funding we need. There are still a few spots left. I'd love for you to close us out. Can I count you in for $1 million?"

Notes on Closing

The Elements of Closing

These are the basic elements of most closes. Keep in mind that not all investors will require you to move through each of these hoops. Some may just want to know where to wire the cash.

Verbal "yes." An investor tells you he or she is in.

Term sheet. You receive a term sheet—a document outlining the basic terms of the agreement. VCs will always give you a term sheet, some angels will, and other funding sources will have different ways of outlining the agreement.

Due diligence. The investor (and you, if you're smart) goes through a formal process of research.

Signatures and money transfer. You sign the final documents and the investor transfers money to your account.

Due Diligence: What Needs to Happen before I Can Close?

The due diligence process changes with every investor, but there are a few common areas you should pay attention to.

Legal and Accounting

From a legal and accounting standpoint, you'll need to make sure you have completed the following steps before you enter a closing conversation. Of course, as with anything law-related, you should always consult a lawyer. (In other words, this is not legal advice, we're not lawyers, don't sue, so on and so forth.)

Incorporate as a Delaware C corporation. The short answer for why you should be a Delaware C is that investors prefer it.

Handle post-incorporation issues. Specifically, set up your articles of incorporation, bylaws, vesting schedules, and intellectual property assignment.

Collect any tax filings and past financial statements, if you have been a company for more than a year.

Get a startup lawyer. Ask the people you meet with which lawyers have good reputations with entrepreneurs in your city. A few big firms are Wilson Sonsini Goodrich & Rosati; Walker Corporate Law Group; and DLA Piper.

Due Diligence Documents

You'll want to gather the following documents.

Financial history. Previous tax filings and any historical income statements.

Articles of incorporation. The proof that you are an official business.

Bylaws. A legal document that describes how decisions are made in the venture.

Org chart. A list of everyone employed in your venture, the roles they play, and who they report to.

Financial model. Twelve months to three years of future revenue and expense projections, along with the assumptions those projections are based on.

Cap table. How the ownership pie of the venture gets split up—a table with a list of owners and the shares each owner has.

Your Due Diligence on the Investor

Due diligence goes both ways. Here are some tools and questions to answer as you research a potential investor.

Places to Research

- LinkedIn

- Gust

- AngelList

- Quora

Questions to Ask Investors

Tell me about a time when a relationship with an entrepreneur you invested in went sour. What happened?

Questions to Ask Their Portfolio Companies

Would you take money from him or her again? What's the biggest asset they brought to the table other than money?

Signatures and Money Transfer

This is the simplest part of the entire fundraising process. Your lawyer will draft the documents you need to sign, you can upload them to an electronic signing service like HelloSign or DocuSign, create a business bank account (if you don't already have one), and send the wiring instructions via e-mail, along with the links to the documents.

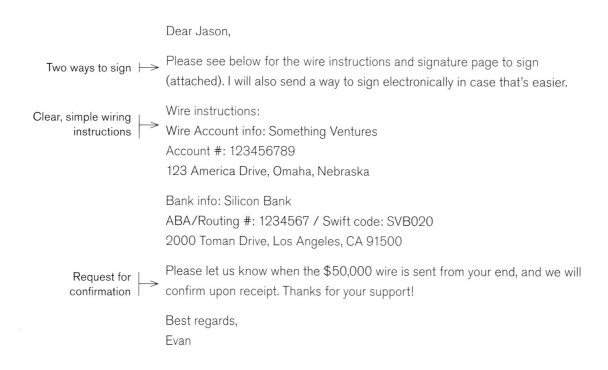

Dear Jason,

Two ways to sign ⟼ Please see below for the wire instructions and signature page to sign (attached). I will also send a way to sign electronically in case that's easier.

Clear, simple wiring instructions ⟼ Wire instructions:
Wire Account info: Something Ventures
Account #: 123456789
123 America Drive, Omaha, Nebraska

Bank info: Silicon Bank
ABA/Routing #: 1234567 / Swift code: SVB020
2000 Toman Drive, Los Angeles, CA 91500

Request for confirmation ⟼ Please let us know when the $50,000 wire is sent from your end, and we will confirm upon receipt. Thanks for your support!

Best regards,
Evan

Conclusion

by Evan Baehr

I have always been passionate about changing the world around me—bringing it into conformity with a vision for society in which more people flourish. For much of my youth, that passion was expressed through law and politics. Everyone I saw on television who was talking about "the world around us" was a lawyer or politician. So I followed what I knew and headed into debate and law with an aspiration for politics and public policy.

I joined the Woodrow Wilson School of Public and International Affairs at Princeton, worked at major think tanks, the White House, and the United States Congress. And what I saw in front of me was decades of "paying your dues," slowly working your way into more and more influence in a system based on seniority and who you know rather than excellence and creativity. The system I was part of exerted tremendous influence on society, but I had no agency in it.

Along the way I met a fascinating man named Peter Thiel, with whom I went on to launch a company. His worldview and life experience taught me that entrepreneurship is a valid and, arguably, preferable means to change society. Twenty years earlier, Peter had shared many of the passions I had; as an undergraduate at Stanford, Peter had founded *The Stanford Review*, the sister publication to *The Princeton Tory*, the paper I edited as a senior. Peter went on to law school but soon developed a passion for entrepreneurship and technology, going on to found PayPal and later invest in and build Palantir, Facebook, SpaceX, and Airbnb—companies that radically transformed society.

Each of these companies began with a vision for transforming society by asking:

- What can we do to stop the bad monetary policies of the Federal Reserve? Create an international currency (PayPal).

- What can we do to accelerate human exploration and discovery of space? Create a better, faster way to launch rockets (SpaceX).

- What can we do to break the unionized taxi commissions that have created a horrible transportation experience? Let anyone be a driver (Lyft).

- What can we do to stop terrorist attacks on the United States? Build world-class data analysis and visualization technology based on antifraud online payments algorithms (Palantir).

Earlier in my life, I would have offered very different answers to those questions, including run for office, write a white paper, publish a book, lobby congress, and so on. I now believe that entrepreneurship is a more effective way to transform society, more thoroughly and more quickly.

A classic definition of entrepreneurship is "marshaling resources beyond your immediate control." During the first minutes of a new idea, you are alone with it. In front of you is a huge challenge to bring others alongside this idea, initially as conversation partners to give feedback and later as partners. Entrepreneurship is the act of cultivating and harnessing resources to bring an idea to fruition, ideally in a scalable, profitable business model.

Entrepreneurship is more than a mere presentation of facts. After all, nothing happens in the world without something first being sold. And the most effective way to sell—whether recruiting employees, raising investments, or acquiring customers—is to tell a story. This is why I fell in love with pitch decks.

Pitch decks are the initial *how* of entrepreneurship; they provide the context, framework, and narrative for how you marshal resources beyond your control—resources like funding, feedback, and, most importantly, relationships.

Recruiting and harnessing resources beyond our immediate control is the *what* of entrepreneurship. Pitch decks are the beginning of the *how*. And profoundly transforming the society around us so that we may more deeply flourish is the *why* of entrepreneurship. And, if you accept its invitation, you are its *who*.

Bringing Ideas to Life

Launching a venture is about attempting, often against great odds, to create the future of which you want to be part. It's extremely difficult to do that without cash. It's impossible without relationships. We believe deeply that entrepreneurship is a social good. Entrepreneurs hold the keys to innovation, new job creation, and deep, personal fulfillment. That is, if they are courageous (or should that be crazy?) enough to give it a try.

There's a good chance you've already been crazy enough to try or plan to be very soon. As we think about the ups and downs of our own journeys, the triumph and defeat, the words of President Teddy Roosevelt have consistently reminded us of what we believe to be most true.

It is not the critic who counts; not the man who points out how the strong man stumbles, or where the doer of deeds could have done them better. The credit belongs to the man who is actually in the arena, whose face is marred by dust and sweat and blood; who strives valiantly; who errs, who comes short again and again, because there is no effort without error and shortcoming; but who does actually strive to do the deeds; who knows great enthusiasms, the great devotions; who spends himself in a worthy cause; who at the best knows in the end the triumph of high achievement, and who at the worst, if he fails, at least fails while daring greatly, so that his place shall never be with those cold and timid souls who neither know victory nor defeat.

See you in the arena.

Index

following up, 187, 206

fonts, 54, 57

format of text, 65, 68

founders, common mistakes by, 74, 78, 82, 86, 90, 94, 98, 102, 106, 110, 114, 118, 122, 126, 130

Freight Farms, 98–101

frequently asked questions (FAQs) slides, 34, 201

Friedman, Jonathan, 98

friends and family, funding from, 10, 155

friendship loop, 167–171, 177

friendships, 5

  building with investors, 191

  leapfrogging with, 184–187

  social graph of, 175–178

fundraising, 5–6

  from accelerators, 154, 157

  from angel investors, 1, 10, 148, 154, 158–163

  creating connections and, 45–47

  crowdfunding, 10, 147, 154, 156

equity financing agreements and, 149–151

four ways of, 146–147

from friends and family, 10, 155

friendship loop in, 167–171

friendships in, 5

history of for startups, 10–13

introductions in, 173–187

learning skills for, 4–5

primer on startup, 145–152

questions to ask before, 166

rounds in, 148–149

snares in, 168

sources for, 153–171

through borrowing, 146

through donations, 147

through profits, 146

through selling equity, 147

types of capital in, 4

unexpected miracles in, 5

from venture capital firms, 10, 12, 148–149, 154, 164

Gaal, Robert, 106

gifts, 205, 207–208

GM, 11

Goldsmith, Jonathan, 196

Gong, Sam, 110

go-to-market strategy, 37

Graham, Kevin, 130

Graham, Paul, 12–13, 149, 174

gratitude, 196–197, 205

gridlines, 56

growth plans, 36

growth stage, 154

Gust, 221

haiku pitch, 139

hard charger asks, 219

Harrison, Scott, 39–41

  customer stories of, 43–45

  industry story of, 45–47

  origin story of, 40–43

  venture growth story of, 47–49

Haughey, Chris, 126

Haughey, Will, 126

Heath, Chip, 212

Heath, Dan, 212

Heddleston, Russ, 90

hero's journey stories, 42, 43

The Hero with a Thousand Faces (Campbell), 43

Hinge, 102–105

history slides, 34, 37

hockey-stick graphs, 24

Hopkins, Adam, 176

how it works slides, 36

hue, 58

iContact, 82

IdeaPaint, 165, 190

IDEO, 167

imagery, 67, 68

images and photography, 35–36, 54, 58, 59–61

  as backgrounds, 61

  charts, 62

  five ways of showing, 62–63

  flowcharts, 63

  maps, 62

  portraits, 62

  resolution of, 61

  stock, 60–61

tone of text, 65, 67–68

To Sell Is Human (Pink), 189

total addressable market (TM), 26–27

traction

slides, 23–24

storytelling on, 52

TreeHouse Home Improvement, 1–2, 5, 130–133, 158, 191, 198

elevator pitch of, 18

trends, 20

trust, 170, 182

building with investors, 191

e-mail script for building, 183

first impressions and, 192–193

transfers of, 170, 182, 196

Twitter, 71, 179, 194

typography, 54, 57. *See also* text

Unsplash, 60–61

US Department of Defense, 11

use cases, 22

use of funds slides, 33–34

valuation, pre-money/post-money, 150

valuation slides, 38

value proposition, 37, 44, 82

van Wel, Steven, 106, 200–201

Varshavskaya, Deena, 4, 215

venture capital, 10, 12, 148–149, 154, 164

Venture Deals (Feld & Mendelson), 149

venture growth stories, 47–49, 52

vesting, 150

vision, 14, 18, 35, 223–224

voice in writing, 65, 67–68

Wall Street Journal, 13

Wanelo, 4, 215

Washington, Joel, 118

weak ties, in social graphs, 178

Where Good Ideas Come From (Johnson), 177

Williamson, Brian, 130

Winshall, Walt, 136

Wired magazine, 12–13

Wish, Joel, 122

word choice, 67

Word documents, 72

working with people you like, 219

writing style, 65–66

X Prize Foundation, 167

Yanosy, Paul, 130

Y Combinator, 12–13, 149, 157, 174

"Your Business Plan Isn't a Fundraising Tool Anymore" (Lee), 13

About the Authors

EVAN BAEHR is the cofounder of Able, a tech company committed to growing the "fortune five million" small businesses around the United States with collaborative, low-interest loans. He's worked at the White House, a hedge fund, and Facebook and is a graduate of Princeton, Yale, and Harvard Business School.

EVAN LOOMIS loves helping startups launch and raise capital. He heads up Corporate Strategy at Corinthian Health Services and is the founder of Tradecraft, a consultancy for high-growth businesses. Evan also mentors entrepreneurs through the accelerators Techstars and Praxis. His first startup was TreeHouse, a first-of-its-kind home improvement store specializing in performance and design. Evan also cofounded Wedgwood Circle, an international angel investment group. Prior to Wedgwood, Evan worked on Wall Street as an investment banker.